# PRAIRIE SOLDIER

By

Richard J. Haase

# Contents

# Dedication

To the courageous men of the 2nd Battalion, 31st Infantry Regiment

# Acknowledgments

Many people helped bring this book to fruition. My son and daughter, Jim and Ann, not only encouraged me and technologically supported me but also filled in occasional factual holes, giving me a way to tell their children, my grandchildren, about my life experience.

I heartily thank LeAne Rutherford and Barbara Jeffus for their diligent editing, formatting, and shepherding of the manuscript into print. They, in turn, thank the editorial staff at Amazon for their professional guidance in readying the book and distributing it.

Reilyn Schoenfelder, an Honors American Studies student at Rochester, Mayo High School, was responsible for rekindling my family's and my interest in this story.

I would be remiss if I did not recognize the influence of my late father, Merwin Haase, himself having served in World War II. He provided me with love and a keen sense of my military responsibilities.

Whether you are a friend or family or just a curious reader, I appreciate your interest in this as-yet unresolved conflict.

Finally, I wholeheartedly thank my wife, Edna, for her encouragement of this endeavor and her partnership in life.

# About the Author

Richard Haase, author of this historical story, *Prairie Soldier*, joined the National Guard in Benson, Minnesota, at an early age—just 17. Two years later, in 1950, he was called up to serve and subsequently, after training, was hand-picked to fight in Korea. Sailing under the Golden Gate Bridge and across the Pacific, he arrived first in Yokohama, Japan, then Inchon, Korea, and finally at a spot in the middle of this embattled nation as a member of the 7th Infantry Division.

40,000 Americans were killed and more than 100,000 wounded in this war which Richard maintains "accomplished nothing." One of the most disastrous battles occurred at Chosin Reservoir near the Yalu River on China's Manchurian border, setting the scene for his book. Arriving in Korea, he was assigned to a rifle company, then later transferred to Battalion S-2 Intelligence Section. Ultimately, he was the section sergeant for the Battalion.

After serving a year in Korea, Richard was able to return home uninjured to a normal life on the Northern Prairie. He completed a Civil Engineering degree, worked in construction, and married. He and his wife have two children and three grandchildren. From cornfield to battlefield and back, his heart always returned to the land.

# Prologue

At the end of World War Two, the people of the United States were on an emotional high. They had emerged from a ruinous economic depression and had engaged in a great crusade. They had come through victorious. All their values stood the test, and they had won. Now they were going to settle down to enjoy a time of peace and prosperity. Like being part of the winning hometown high school team, they had captured the state championship and were now receiving the accolades of the admiring citizens. Everything was going to be just fine.

Oh, there were a few clouds on the horizon, but nobody paid much attention to them. After all, the great and all-powerful United States had exclusive possession of the nuclear shield. Who would dare to challenge a country with this terrible weapon of destruction?

When in the summer of 1950, the armed forces of North Korea rolled across the 38th parallel, many Americans could hardly believe it. Who had the audacity to challenge the "Colossus of the North"? The first U.S. troops on the scene thought the North Koreans would run when they saw the American flag.

The reason that the communist regime of North Korea felt that they could engage in such blatant aggression was simple. The U.S. government had publicly stated that South Korea would not be defended by the Americans in case of an attack. In retrospect, this was a grave miscalculation. It was akin to giving the fox the key to the chicken coop.

In the five years between 1945 and 1950, the US military had undergone a serious decline. From a position as the most powerful military force in history, the uniformed services had steadily deteriorated to a hollow shell. This was especially true of the Army and Marine Corps. Many people believed that the usefulness of ground forces was over.

When the Korean conflict began, there was only a scattering of advisors on the peninsula and four under-strength divisions in the Far East. As the North Korean offensive smashed the poorly trained and ill-equipped South Korean Army, the U.S. divisions were fed into the battle on a piecemeal basis. With a heroic effort, however, the battered American and South Korean forces held a beachhead around the southern port city of Pusan.

In a masterstroke, General Douglas McArthur, the supreme commander in the Far East, landed the 1st Marine Division and the 7th Infantry Division on the west coast of Korea at Inchon. This effectively cut off the overextended North Korean forces and turned their offensive into a disorganized retreat. At that time, an all-out drive was launched with the goal in mind of ending the war and capturing the entire Korean Peninsula. It was then that the men of the 1st Marine Division and the 7th Infantry Division found themselves moving north into the rugged mountains of the Taebaek Range of North Korea near the Chosin Reservoir.

The basic plan was for the 1st Marine Division to secure the town of Hagaru-ri at the south end of the reservoir and then to advance to the northwest. The 7th infantry was ordered to move to Hagaru-ri with a regimental-sized force and advance along the east side of the Chosin Reservoir. These two divisions, which made up the bulk of the X Corps, were poised to continue their rapid but rather disorganized pursuit of the beaten North Korean Army.

Thus, the stage was set for one of the most disastrous actions in U.S. military history and certainly the costliest battle in the history of the 7th Infantry Division. The sudden intervention of the sturdy, disciplined, tenacious soldiers of China's People's Liberation Army was a titanic shock to the U.S. and the Republic of Korea and completely changed their situation. The mode of the army units on the east side of Chosin had gone from pursuing a dispirited enemy to a desperate fight for their own survival. In the space of a few hours, the Chinese forces had not only stopped the 31st Regimental Combat Team (RCT) but had surrounded the unit and cut them off from any hope of relief. It had turned into a "last stand" situation in the classic sense of the words.

In fact, several striking similarities exist between the 31st RCT's fight at Chosin and the 7th U.S. Calvary Regiment's fight at Little Bighorn. These are the similarities:

Both actions were disasters for the army units involved.

Both debacles were brought about by impetuous commanders. In the case of Chosin, this would include General Edward Almond, CO of the X Corps; Colonel Allan D. MacLean, CO, 31st Infantry Regiment; and Lieutenant Colonel Don C. Faith, CO, 1st Battalion, 32nd Infantry. In the case of Little Bighorn, it was General George A. Custer.

Both disasters could have been avoided if more prudent command decisions had been made.

Many unanswered questions remain in each action. For example, why did the forces split up prior to the battle? Most of these questions will probably never be answered.

Both actions were fought by old-line units of the Regular Army.

In both cases, about a third of the command was killed: In Chosin, about 1000 out of 3000; in Little Bighorn, about 250 out of 600.

In both events, the U.S. forces were attacking and, in turn, were attacked by overwhelming odds.

Both actions were ultimately a "last stand situation."

In both cases, the commanders grossly underestimated the strength of the enemy. (General Almond's comment was, "Don't let a bunch of Chinese laundrymen stop you.")

Many of the remains of the men killed in both fights will probably never be found.

Both events were a clash of two diverse cultures and political systems.

Both battles were a result of questionable political decisions and flawed public policy.

The main difference between the two actions is that Little Bighorn has captured the imagination of the American public while Chosin is all but forgotten.

In many ways, the war in Korea was a transition from the age of idealism and innocence to a time of compromise and pragmatism. The U.S. Army of the Korean War had many things in common with the old army of the post-Civil War era and perhaps the colonial period. Here again, was the "thin red line" holding off hordes of enemies who would overrun the "empire." A few individuals existed in the U.S. Army of 1950 who, as young soldiers, had served in World War One and on the Mexican Border. They had seen the dusty columns of horse cavalry in action and had known men who wore the blue uniforms of the Army of the Indian Wars. (It should be noted that the 31st Infantry was the only U.S infantry regiment in the Philippines at the beginning of World War Two. They were forced to surrender to Japanese forces in the Spring of 1942.)

The backdrop of the story is the action of the hastily organized 31st Regimental Combat Team (RCT) during the period from November 26th through December 1st, 1950. All members of the platoon are fictional. The higher commanders mentioned in the story were real. The main character, the young infantry lieutenant from the Northern Plains, is a composite of several individuals, some who could have been participants in the battle and some who were not. The characters of the enlistees of the platoon were based on actual members of the U.S. Infantry during that period.

The story attempts to allow the reader to experience the battle through the eyes of one young infantry officer. It is hoped that the reader will gain some appreciation of the sacrifices and courage of the infantry and artillery soldiers of the 31st RCT. These men who braved the terrible cold and who fought the overwhelming masses of the tough Chinese infantry were truly comrades in spirit with the men of the Alamo, Little Bighorn, and Bataan.

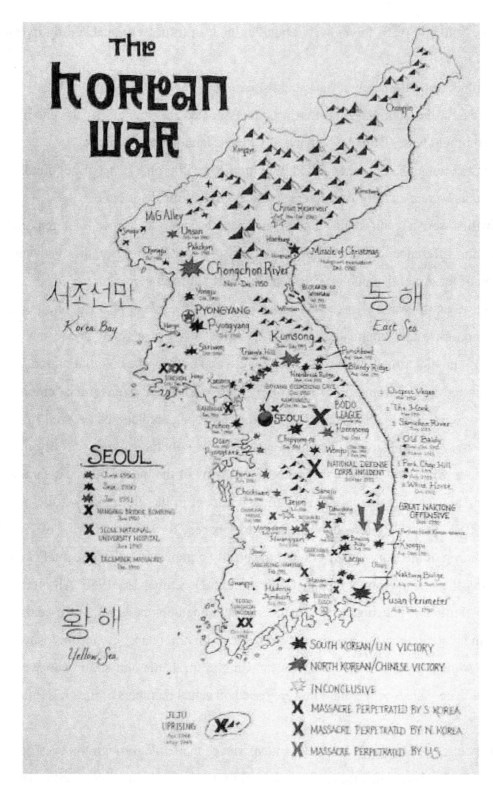

*Korean War Map by and courtesy of Jesse Kennedy, MediaevalMapmaker*

# Harvesting

It had been a tough harvest season on the Northern Plains of Minnesota. The wintry weather had come early, and with it, rain and snow. Only a few days had been suitable for combining. The big machines could roll over many acres in a day when conditions were favorable. But no machine--no matter how immense or sophisticated--could move when the fields had turned to mud. Harvest machines, combines, resemble great prehistoric creatures as they move back and forth over the fields making slow, lumbering turns at the ends of the corn rows. Combines are indeed the leviathans of the prairie doing the work of more than a hundred men and teams. The technology leading toward modern harvesters reaches back to the dawn of time. The spirit of the ancient reaper with a handheld sickle perhaps looks over the massive machines and smiles with approval.

The prairie farmland of the Midwest yields two major crops: corn and soybeans. These crops are planted in the spring, grow to maturity over the summer, and are ready for harvest in the fall. As the air becomes cooler and the days become shorter, the plants dry and turn from a deep green color to shades of brown and tan. Crops ready to harvest possess a certain beauty. Long ranks of stalks stand like an ancient, silent army. Soybeans, which are usually harvested first, emerge from the combine as tan-colored spheres the size of a large shot. Corn kernels are bright yellow seeds about the size of a small fingernail. These two commodities are the major ingredients of animal feed as well as a host of other products. Without corn and beans, the shelves of the world's supermarkets would be Spartan indeed. The Midwest, with the world's most extensive tract of fertile land and with its mechanized farmers, produces corn and soybeans by the shipload.

Light snow was falling over the field of standing corn and the two large combines. The combines were moving, but the wet ground was slowing their progress. An oversized truck stood near the entrance to the field. The truck had two rear axles with dual wheels. The truck box was rectangular with high sides and a canvas top. Periodically one of the combines would drive from the corn rows over to the truck and unload its hopper of shelled corn. The combine would stop alongside the truck, swing out a large auger conveyor, and start filling the truck box. A heavy stream of shelled corn poured from the end of the auger into the open expanse of the truck box.

Even though it was only late afternoon, a grey haze covered the landscape, limiting visibility. The machine operators peered through the safety glass of the cabs' windshields as the rows of cornstalks marched methodically into the gathering chains of the combine headers. Through the

1

gloom, a second truck appeared on the gravel and pulled into the field. The second truck, identical to the first, moved directly behind the standing truck and stopped.

The driver of the second truck opened the cab door, swung out his feet, and looked across the field at the moving combines. He picked up the radio handset that was on a dash-mounted clip. "Are you on, Bill?"

"Yeah."

"How's it going?"

"Still going." After an interval of silence, the truck driver asked, "What do you think?"

The answer from Bill came across the air: "If we get much more snow, we'll be plugged up."

The truck driver spoke over the radio: "Use your best judgment."

"OK."

The driver of the truck stepped carefully down from the cab. He was tall, six feet two inches, medium build, close-cut graying hair, and pale blue eyes. He walked resolutely for his 60-plus years but with a slight limp and a noticeable twist in his left shoulder. John W. Schneidermann was the farm owner. In fact, he owned many farms. He was, like most of the farmers of these northern plains, the master of his domain. His land, machines, and crops were worth several million dollars on the open market, and his debt was minimal. John W. Schneidermann answered to no one.

The business community in the nearby town existed to supply the area farmers with seed, fertilizer, chemicals, machinery, fuel, and money. When John Schneidermann came into the bank, the president came out of his office and extended a respectful greeting: "Good to see you, John. Come on into the office."

The family had a long history with the land. William Heinrich Schneidermann was born in 1839 in what Germany is now. At age sixteen, he emigrated to the United States with an uncle, settling in southern Minnesota. The lush prairies were teeming with activity, and the young men soon found profitable work. In the fall of 1862, a terrible conflict broke out, pitting the European settlers against the Santee Sioux. William Schneidermann joined an army unit and served for two years in Minnesota and the Dakota Territory. At age twenty-five, he married and acquired a 160-acre farm.

In 1867, on the home farm, James P. Schneidermann was born. He worked on the farm and eventually purchased two quarter sections of land. In 1895, he married, and the following year welcomed a new son, August.

August H. Schneidermann grew up on the fertile farmland of southern Minnesota. In 1919, he married a neighbor girl after returning home from France, where he served in the 165th Infantry, 42nd Division of the American Expedition Forces, and fought the Kaiser's army, which undoubtedly included some relatives. In 1928, John William Schneidermann was also born on the home farm, which then had grown to six quarter sections, about 960 acres.

The Schneidermann family had several traits that seemed to carry over from generation to generation. One was the love of the land. When a new piece of land was acquired, the incentive was to hold it for the long pull. Another characteristic was the ability of the family to work together. This is somewhat rare among Northern Europeans because most family farming operations last three generations at most. A third common family trait was that of thrift and hard work, which usually go hand in hand. The Schneidermann family knew the value of a dollar. Even after they became comparatively well off, they never thought of themselves as rich. Instead, they had this driving urge to save and, above all, to do a "good day's work."

Consequently, while many Midwestern farms fell victim to the boom-and-bust cycle of agriculture, the Schneidermann family managed to hold on in bad times and to make modest advances in good times. Their family loyalty, patriotism, and persistent efforts paid off in the long run. And so it was that John Schneidermann, along with several other family members, owned a substantial number of acres of rich, black Minnesota land.

It is probable that the forces that shaped these individuals had their origins in the cramped, repressive conditions in Europe. These conditions, typical of the German states of yesteryear, condemned farmers to the status of poor peasants. When the settlers saw the vast, rich lands of the Midwest, they knew they had arrived at a modern Eden.

John Schneidermann stood by the truck he had just parked. A dog stood on the edge of the seat and looked down at the ground. "Come on, Fritz." The dog, a silver and black shepherd scrambled down the steps of the cab. The driver walked to the rear of the massive truck, unlatched a long crank arm, and unrolled the tarp covering the top of the box. The snow had all but stopped, and the air was clearing. John Schneidermann stood alongside the silent truck and surveyed the two machines as they marched through the tan ranks of the standing corn stalks. The picked stalks covered the ground like a crazy quilt. The dark black soil, now streaked with snow, was visible between the remnants of the corn rows.

One of the combines was moving toward the trucks, its bank of lights blazing. The big machine appeared lifelike as it crunched through the broken corn stalks. The combine then moved beside the first truck as the unloading auger swung out. Soon the powerful diesel engine, the heart of the harvester, speeded up. A bright stream of shelled corn poured from the end of the auger spout into the empty truck box, which began filling rapidly. The machine moved backward in slow jerks, each time filling that part of the truck to capacity. As the lead truck filled, the auger stopped, and the combine backed to a position alongside the second truck. The engine again speeded up, and corn again started cascading into the empty truck box. The combine engine again speeded up, and the unloading auger swung to the side of the machine like an oversized bird's wing. The harvester moved off to join its teammate slowly, deliberately.

John Schneidermann walked to the rear of the first truck, worked the long crank, and rolled out the tarp covering the big grain box like a tent. The crank arm locked in place, stretching the tarp cover to a taut, wrinkle-free top. The combine was now back to its place in the standing corn devouring eight rows of corn as it moved through the field. From the rear of the square body of the machine, a steady stream of corn cobs and husks dropped to the ground. The farmer slowly walked to the front of the forward truck and climbed the steps of the cab. In response to a whistle, Fritz bounced over, climbed the steps of the truck, and hopped into the cab.

The F-850 Ford truck was a massive unit with ten tires on the ground. The cab was spacious, and the dash had an array of dials. Two crooked shifting levers were positioned on the floor of the cab. The driver turned the key, and after a few revolutions, the engine started with a roar. The driver turned the knob operating the windshield wipers knocking a layer of snow off the glass. The clutch pedal was depressed, and the lower gear engaged. The engine revolutions increased, the clutch pedal slowly released, and the big truck grudgingly began to move forward. With a weight of fifteen tons of grain, the wheels of the truck pressed into the wet surface of the field, forming a track. The gears of the transmission whined as the truck slowly crawled up the field entrance and onto the gravel road.

# Moving Out

The gears of the truck whined as the road became steeper. Second Lieutenant John W. Schneidermann sat in the rider's side of the cab and looked out on the desolate Korean landscape.

"You might not see any shooting at all, Lieutenant. I hear we might be back in Japan by Christmas."

"You might be right."

"I hope so. You know it was sure nice in Japan. You been in Japan, Lieutenant?"

"Just passed through." The truck driver was a lanky private from Arkansas. "We sure put the run on the gooks. The Inchon landing did it. You have to hand it to old Mac for that."

"I guess that's right."

"I see you've got an M-1, Lieutenant. Don't you like carbines?"

"Well, I am partial to a rifle, but I have a .45, too."

Second Lieutenant John W. Schneidermann balanced an M-1 rifle in an upright position, its butt on the steel floor of the truck cab. He had traded his issued carbine for a rifle at a supply tent at the division rear. It was a sleek, new weapon, recently unpacked. Some traces remained of the thick, heavy cosmoline grease that all weapons were packed in at the arsenal.

Schneidermann was able to sight-in his new rifle during his short stay at the port. The East Coast ports of Korea were congested, bustling places as the elements of the U.S Army's X Corps were unloading and heading north in the Fall of 1950. It was an impressive sight to a young infantry replacement, a second lieutenant.

The term "replacement" has an unsettling sound. A replacement is an orphan until becoming part of an existing outfit. John Schneidermann had joined a company just two days before. It was a typical rifle company of that time with three rifle platoons, a weapons platoon with 60 mm mortars and 57 mm recoilless, and a company headquarters group. The company at strength numbered about 190 men altogether, including about 50 ROKs (Republic of Korea soldiers).

The miles slowly rolled by as the convoy climbed the twisting roads through narrow passes and around massive peaks. This was rough terrain leading into the heart of the Taebaek Mountain Range, a harsh environment for the mechanized soldiers of the 7th Infantry Division. Occasionally the trucks would stop, letting the men out to stretch and exercise in an effort to restore warmth to feet and hands. The men of the battalion would climb back aboard their trucks and, after the usual confusion, would start up the road to the north. There were a few signs of habitation, mud huts with thatched roofs. Occasionally a group of small buildings would seem to be a village, or so the name on the map implied.

After two more hours on the snow-covered roads, the village of Hagaru-ri came into view. This town was located near the south end of the Chosin (Changjin) Reservoir, a narrow, artificial lake perched between several mountain ranges. At Hagaru-ri, the road forked, one branch going west and the other east. The battalion turned east and headed along the shore of the reservoir. After about five miles, the trucks pulled into an area just south of a hill mass designated as 1221, the map elevation in meters. The road continued to the north.

The bivouac area was not the most hospitable: uninviting terrain, snow on the ground, and cold temperatures. At night the mercury had been dropping below zero degrees Fahrenheit. The men dismounted from the unheated trucks, climbing down the tailgates. As the various platoons gathered, a runner from the company Command Post (CP) approached the lieutenant and his command group. "Platoon leaders and sergeants report to the company CP."

"I guess that means us, Lieutenant."

Platoon sergeant Pratt was a confident individual: thirty-eight years old, a veteran of the Pacific fighting in World War II, and a man comfortable with himself. Sergeant First Class Thomas C. Pratt had been in the company longer than all but three other men. A native of the Texas Hill Country, he had grown up knowing the meaning of the word "poor." He had enlisted in the army in 1930 and was glad to have the job. At sixteen dollars a month minus certain charges such as laundry, he said he "never got rich," but he got along. Thomas C. Pratt liked soldiering. He liked the security and stability, and he liked the authority of a non-com in the pre-war army. The men tended to like Thomas C. Pratt. He had a way of showing quiet determination and maintaining an air of command.

The company commander was forward along the line of parked trucks. He was sitting in the seat of the command jeep with the executive officer standing against the canvas top of the vehicle. He said, "Well, men, this is it for the night. We will occupy the positions left by the Marines. The CP will be just north and a little west of where we are now. All of the rifle platoons will be on the line according to this overlay that I will pass out. The kitchen is going to try and set up a hot meal a little later. Tomorrow the order is to attack north and on to the Yalu. Are there any questions?"

6

The platoon leaders and sergeants scattered, each heading back to his respective unit.

"I'll try and get these guys moved out to their positions, Lieutenant. Maybe we should have a squad leaders' meeting first, Sarge."

"Yeah, that would probably be all right, sir. I'll round them up."

John Schneidermann thought: *I didn't want to discourage him. He has been pretty helpful to a brand-new shavetail. He could use his experience to make me look like a rookie.... The terrain sure looks desolate--a little like Minnesota in the winter but more rugged. The cold is beginning to get severe. We are going to have to look out for frostbite.*

"The squad leaders are ready, Sir."

"Thanks, Sergeant."

"Men, we are going to be here for tonight. Our line will be over to our right. All squads will be on the line, including the two light .30s. We will be attacking north sometime tomorrow, so this won't be permanent. The Marines seem to think that the gooks are quite a way to the north. The position looks pretty good, so it won't take much digging.

Another thing. Wipe off the excess oil from your weapons. Fuel oil works about as good as anything. When it's cold like this, bolts freeze if there is excess oil. Let's go. Sergeant Pratt and I will locate the squad positions. There will be hot chow later. Remember those weapons. Cold weather can really lock up those bolts."

# Frozen

The cold was getting worse. John Schneidermann was slowly moving across the frozen, snow-covered field. He had set out after school toward the low tree line that marked the river's location. Foxes lived in those woods; a fox is a worthy adversary. They are smart with sharp senses. When you hunt foxes with a rifle by yourself, you are on their terms--so different from those big drives when a gang of hunters surround a section of land and then slowly walk toward the center. That is a way to get game, but it's not the same as meeting animals one on one.

The old Winchester Model 90 was a classic, a slide action repeater with an open hammer. It shot a Remington Special cartridge, like a .22 rifle but about half again as long.

The sun was setting behind the tree line, and the daylight was rapidly fading. The wind was still, but the temperature was dropping. Hands and feet are always the first to freeze, even when wearing shoepacs and lined gloves.

The fox had been crouching in the fence line. For some reason, inexperience or impulse, the young fox decided to make a run for it. The eyes of the young hunter and the fox met for a brief second. The hunter and the hunted were in one flash of time on equal terms. John Schneidermann instinctively raised his rifle and, at a range of 40 yards, fired. A tuft of snow raised just over and beyond the fox. The hunter tried to work the bolt, but nothing happened. The oil in the weapon and the intense cold had locked the bolt in place. The fox ran in a straight line for the safety of the woods, to live another day.

# Cold Comfort

The platoon began trooping into the previously built fortifications. This was a break for the infantrymen as the top few inches of ground were starting to freeze solid. The platoon leader, along with the platoon sergeant, made a walking tour of the infantry line. They checked each position for fields of fire, ammunition supply, and the condition of the weapons. "Make sure your weapons are dry and clean."

"

Hey, Lieutenant, those gooks won't stop running 'til they hit the Yalu. You'll be lucky if you get to see one."

"Maybe you're right, but I still like to see a weapon that will fire."

The camp area took on a habitable appearance as the troops began preparing for the coming darkness. Campfires sent up circling columns of smoke. The kitchen stoves, with their bright, clean, blue flames, gave a homey air to the mess tents. Men were moving back and forth within the perimeter.

"If it wasn't so damn cold, it wouldn't be too bad," was the feeling of the men in the ranks. The hot supper helped raise everyone's spirits. The steaming coffee and the hot stew were well-received.

The terrain was stark and austere. The snow-covered reservoir, the mountain peaks visible in all directions, and the scrum trees all combined to create a grim, forbidding landscape. To many of the soldiers of the 7th Infantry Division, especially those from urban areas, the bleak outlook was depressing. To Lieutenant John Schneidermann, who grew up in the rural heartland, the terrain was not really that menacing. It had a certain similarity to parts of the Midwest. In 1863 and 1864, the men of the army expeditions against the Sioux might have had the same feelings.

The company was a diverse group. Most of the officers and senior non-coms were veterans of World War II. In addition, boys just out of high school had recently joined the regular army for an adventure. The Republic of Korea (ROK) soldiers made up a significant part of the company. These were mostly untrained young men who had been conscripted by Syngman Rhee's military police.

John Schneidermann thought as he looked over the platoon position, "A replacement second lieutenant does a lot of observing and listening. You try and get along but do the right thing. These guys have seen some combat, so they must know what they are doing. It's funny how training exercises don't fit the actual situation--the school solution that they taught at the Infantry School; the proper way things should be done."

In his mind, he pictured a plain, white marker: HERE LIE THE BONES OF LT. JONES, A GRADUATE OF THIS INSTITUTION. HE LOST THE FIGHT IN THE MIDDLE OF THE NIGHT, USING THE SCHOOL SOLUTION.

As daylight began to fade, the encampment became quiet. Each man had found the position that he would occupy for the night. Second Lieutenant John Schneidermann silently walked to the platoon CP (Command Post) located about twenty yards behind the middle rifle squad. It was a well-constructed bunker that the Marines had built. The emplacement was a trench dug into the ground with a cover of logs and earth. With a short trench outside, a canvas flap served as a door.

The command group consisted of the platoon leader, the platoon sergeant, the assistant platoon sergeant, a runner, and a medic. They could nicely fit into the CP with a little room to spare. The lieutenant lifted the canvas flap and looked in.

"Come on in, Sir. All the comforts of home." Sergeant Pratt was heating a cup of C-Ration coffee over a pocket gas stove. A sound-powered phone on the wall provided a communication link with the company CP. At the platoon CP, the atmosphere was relaxed. The sturdy shelter was homelike.

Sergeant Pratt called the company CP and reported in. "The squads are all in position, and everything is quiet."

The sound the little gas stove gave off was distinctive, a sort of roar as the pressurized gas rushed to the blue flame of the single burner. These stoves were something of a luxury. It took a certain amount of skill and a little luck to keep them operating.

The platoon sergeant spoke up, "I told the squad leaders to have at least two men awake at all times in each squad if that meets with your approval, Sir."

John Schneidermann could detect a hint of sarcasm in the sergeant's manner, but he didn't want to make an issue of it. "That sounds like a good plan to me, Sergeant." Two could play that game, but the lieutenant had no desire to alienate his right-hand man.

"What is your recommendation on the CP?"

"Well, I would suggest that one of us five be awake at all times. If we break it up into two-hour shifts starting at 2000 Hours, we will each stand one turn."

"Sounds good to me, Sergeant. Put me down for midnight to 0200 if you want to," the platoon leader replied.

"OK, Sir."

"Let's all get some shuteye. Polowski, you take the first shift and wake up Garza at 2200. Ridehout, you take the 0200 to 0400. I'll take the last pull. At 0600, we should all be up anyway unless the skipper decides to make it earlier."

Sergeant Charles E. Ridehout, the assistant platoon sergeant, was a quiet individual. He was always present and always dependable. "Steady" would be a one-word description of the man. An outer shell to his personality existed that no one was able to crack, and therefore no one tried. He hailed from rural Pennsylvania. Sergeant Ridehout knew about hard work and was scrupulously honest. He received very few letters. Sergeant at the end of World War II, Ridehout had enlisted in the Regular Army and had been promoted on a normal basis.

The CP was large enough to hold the five men. Because of the compact nature of the bunker and a makeshift stove, the temperature was bearable. The gap in the canvas door allowed for a generous amount of outside air. The stove, which had been constructed by the former occupants, was jury-rigged from a steel ordinance container of some sort. It even had a short chimney poking up through the roof of the CP. The runner had started a small fire using an assortment of cardboard and twigs. The one-burner gas stove was shut off, leaving the single candle set in a tin can to give off a soft, faint light.

PFC Polowski, the runner, hunkered down, getting ready for his two-hour shift while the other men slipped into their mountain sleeping bags. The runner gave a low whistle into the mouthpiece of the sound-powered phone. "CP, CP, are you on?"

"Go ahead."

"This is third platoon checking in, everything quiet."

Second Lieutenant John W. Schneidermann awoke slowly.

"Wake up, Lieutenant. It's midnight."

"Thanks, Garza. Anything happening?"

"Real quiet, Sir. A couple of shots about a half hour ago, west of us. That was all. I checked with the company, but they said it was nothing. The phone's working, and I have been reporting in every half hour."

John Schneidermann crawled out of his warm sleeping bag. The cold grabbed him like a giant hand reaching into his very being. He picked up the phone. "This is Schneidermann at third platoon. All is quiet." The voice on the other end of the sound-powered phone seemed far away. "I am going out to check the line".

"Be careful, Lieutenant."

The night was overcast with a light breeze. The cold bit with increased ferocity. The lieutenant stood up as he crawled through the canvas door. *Man, it sure is cold--kind of like Minnesota in the winter*, he thought.

The nearest squad position was only about twenty yards away. The platoon leader waited for a few minutes, listening and letting his night vision develop. It was a wild scene here in the mountains of Asia. The rough terrain made it difficult to move around. The shadows seemed to shift; outlines of sinister shapes appeared to be everywhere. *Get hold of yourself. You're supposed to be in charge here,* the platoon leader thought.

John Schneidermann covered the twenty yards in a slow, deliberate walk, listening and looking as he moved along.

No movement or challenge. The sound of breathing and light snoring drifted from the position. The first position was larger than usual, with space for three riflemen. The trench line came into view with the familiar outline of a typical infantry position. Three figures were sprawled within the confines of the emplacement. The platoon leader slowly and deliberately walked to the edge of the trench.

Lieutenant John Schneidermann moved to the next position and to the one next to that. The entire squad was sleeping. The lieutenant moved to the inert form of the squad leader and gripped his shoulder. The squad leader jumped and gave a soft gasp.

"What in the hell is going on, Sergeant? Every man in your whole squad is sound asleep."

"I am sorry, Sir."

"There are supposed to be two men in each squad awake at all times."

"Yes, Sir."

12

The lieutenant checked the other three squads. In one squad, all the men were asleep, another had one man on guard, and the machine gun position had two men awake and alert. The platoon leader thought, "Sergeant Pratt is going to be busy in the morning."

Second Lieutenant John Schneidermann mused as he made his way slowly back to the platoon CP. *What do you do with men who can't take guard duty seriously? In the Civil War, they shot sentries for sleeping on guard.* The CP was just as he left it--four sleeping forms covering the floor area. Phoning in, "This is the 3rd Platoon reporting in. All quiet."

"10-4, Lieutenant, all quiet here, too." The first sergeant's voice came in clear over the sound-powered phone.

The usual clutter lay around the interior of the bunker. Rifles and cartridge belts are stacked along the wall with shoepacs, parkas, helmets, rucksacks, and a duffle bag. The inside of the shelter had the appearance and odor of a hunting camp. The platoon leader crawled back out through the canvas door and out into the night air. The cold still had a sharp bite and, driven by the wind, seemed to creep into every pore.

The manual, *FM 7-10, RIFLE COMPANY, INFANTRY REGIMENT,* held all the techniques that go into leading small infantry units. The methods are those that are used in the attack and defense. Everything is there in neat packages, the sketches, the pictures. They all look easy on paper.

Second Lieutenant John W. Schneidermann reflected, *this weather sure is cold, but Minnesota has weather just as cold--maybe a little colder. Sleeping outside makes a big difference.*

The winter uniform began with a two-piece suit of long-handled winter underwear topped by a wool shirt and pants and then field pants and a wool sweater. A pile jacket under a field jacket made up the outer layer. The foot gear was the shoepac, a north country product made up of a boot with a leather upper and a rubber bottom. Some men in the 32nd Infantry wore regular leather boots and rubber overshoes which was an excellent combination. Two pairs of wool socks were even better, but it was not always possible to have two pairs of dry socks. A pair of leather gloves with wool liners, a wool scarf, and a pile cap rounded out the outfit. The pile cap with its upturned front and sides was the jaunty trademark of the Korean War. Some individuals also had parkas with hoods. Steel helmets were issued to all personnel, but not everyone wore one.

The night continued to be overcast with little starlight. The view from the platoon command post was limited. The elusive dark shapes and shadows were still there. Second Lieutenant John

W. Schneidermann stood peering into the darkness. 0100. Time passed slowly at this part of the night. Time to think. If it wasn't so cold, it would be tolerable.

After some time, the platoon leader ducked back into the CP shelter. The four sleeping forms were still there, and the flickering candle cast a dim yellow light on the silent scene.

For the next hour, John Schneidermann sat in the CP. The other four men slumbered on, emitting a variety of sounds. Some snores, some incoherent talk, and rhythmic breathing gave evidence that all was well. The platoon leader, at intervals of about twenty to thirty minutes, called the company CP reporting that all was quiet. There was a comfortable feeling in hearing a friendly voice. On one such call, the company commander responded to the whistle. "Anything happening on your end, Schneidermann?"

"No, Sir, no problem here."

The company commander continued, "Is everyone awake that is supposed to be?"

The lieutenant replied, "There was a little problem, Sir, but we handled it."

"You might have to kick some butts. Some of these guys think that they are on a picnic and don't have to stay on the ball."

"Yes, Sir."

The candle cast a sputtering light on the dirt walls of the bunker. The cold kept reaching in, reminding the soldiers of their human frailties.

John Schneidermann looked at his M-1 rifle leaning against log support. It was a masterpiece of modern craftsmanship. The walnut wood stock, the dull steel that made up the barrel, the receiver, the trigger guard, and the gas cylinder. It was indeed a handsome weapon, if a rifle can be called handsome. At times an infantryman's rifle is his connection to reality. He takes care of it: taking it apart, cleaning it, and making sure it is in working order. For some individuals, the care becomes a ritual that they blindly perform even in the face of calamity. A rifle is a soldier's key to survival. "Take care of your weapon, and it will take care of you."

# A Good Buy

The hardware store in the rural Minnesota town was well stocked to serve the needs of the prairie farmers and their families with items for their homes and farms. The wide variety of merchandise ranged from nails and bolts to household chemicals. In the sporting goods section, several used rifles stood on a rack behind the counter. John Schneidermann kept looking at a certain weapon at the right end of the rack.

"Well, John, that's a fine-looking weapon," the clerk observed. "They don't make 'em like that anymore. Look at that octagon barrel. You know this rifle has really been taken care of. Just check the bore. Not a trace of rust; it's in beautiful shape. The finish is almost perfect. You know that $35.00 is a good buy!"

The store clerk was a redheaded kid of twenty-five with a bad complexion. He operated on the theory that salesmanship was a major part of success and that you had to talk to sell. "Tell you what, John, I know you need that rifle. You give me five dollars, and I'll put it away for you; give you a chance to get your finances in order, OK?"

John stared at the gun thoughtfully. The clerk kept up a steady dialogue, "How are things in high school? It must be fun with all those pretty girls."

John Schneidermann finally spoke, "Let's go with the deal."

In the grove, John had laid out a practice range. Fifty feet, a hundred feet, and a hundred yards. A piece of 2x12 plank with a bottom piece to make it stand upright served as a target. The Winchester Model 90 was a quality rifle and in good condition. After many days of practice, the proud owner could hit a pop bottle cap at a hundred feet. At age 15, John Schneidermann was an accomplished rifleman.

# Waiting

The hands of the army issue wristwatch turned slowly--0130, 0200, 0230. The platoon leader reached over to where Sergeant Ridehout, the assistant platoon sergeant, was curled up into a cocoon. He gently shook the sergeant by the shoulder. The sergeant made a quick start, "What, what?"

"Time to roll out, Sergeant."

"OK, Lieutenant, be with you in a minute." The assistant platoon sergeant fumbled for the zipper and finally opened his sleeping bag. "Looks like you gave me an extra half hour, Sir."

"That's OK, Sergeant, you didn't mind, did you?"

"No, Sir. I never turn down extra shuteye."

"Everything is pretty quiet. I think I'll go and check the line".

This time the platoon was in full compliance with the guard schedule. Two men were awake in each squad area. Second Lieutenant John Schneidermann slowly walked the twenty yards back to the platoon CP. His M-1 rifle was slung upside down on his right shoulder, fully loaded with an eight-round clip. Conveniently, the ammunition for the M-1 rifle came packed in eight-round clips in cloth bandoliers. A bandolier has six pockets, each containing one clip making it easy for Schneidermann to quickly grab a bandolier and sling it over his shoulder. Second Lieutenant John Schneidermann moved at a deliberate and careful pace. Walking around an infantry line company at night was not the safest thing in the world to be doing.

Back at the CP, the assistant platoon sergeant was sitting up with the phone in his hand. "How are things on the line, Sir?"

"Everything is OK, Sergeant," the lieutenant replied. "I think I'll try and get a little sleep."

The down-filled sleeping bag was a marvelous piece of equipment. Light and durable, above all, it was very warm. Once inside the bag, John Schneidermann drifted off into a fitful sleep. It was still dark when Sergeant Pratt shook the platoon leader.

"What time is it, Sergeant?"

"About 0500 hours, Sir," the sergeant replied. "

"That was a short night! What's up?"

"The company commander wants to see all the officers in twenty minutes."

"OK, Sergeant, I'm on my way. You know, this soldiering wouldn't be so bad if they kept better hours. By the way, I checked the line after midnight, and only four men were awake. I suggest that you look into the matter."

"I'll do just that, Sir, right away," the platoon sergeant replied.

The platoon leader struggled free of his sleeping bag, sat up, and began pulling on his boots. The single-burner stove was still in the middle of the dirt floor, giving off its characteristic blue flame and making its usual roaring noise. A canteen cup of C-Ration coffee sat steaming on the single burner.

"How about a shot of brew, Lieutenant?"

"Thanks, Sergeant. I could sure use some."

Sergeant Pratt lifted the cup off the burner and passed it to the platoon leader. After pouring about half the contents into his own canteen cup, the lieutenant took a sip. "Man, that's good! I didn't think anything could taste that good."

Second Lieutenant John Schneidermann grabbed his rifle, put on his pistol belt, and ducked through the canvas flap. The darkness was complete, like outer space without stars. Slowly the platoon leader's night vision returned as he stood silent and still in the biting cold. After a few minutes, the lieutenant started down a narrow path that led to the company CP, which was set up in a small clay and thatch building.

About 200 yards away, the company CP gave the impression of being a business-like place. In the middle of the largest of three small rooms was a table topped with a Coleman gas lantern which was giving off a brilliant light. Seated around the table, relaxed, were the officers of the company. While the normal complement of officers for a rifle company was six: four platoon leaders, an executive officer, and the company commander, this time, there were only five. The executive officer had been sent back with an injury three weeks earlier. The first sergeant was there in his role as the senior enlisted man of the company.

"Nice you could make it, Schneidermann," said a fellow platoon leader with a grin. Second Lieutenant John W. Schneidermann just smiled and looked down at his watch.

The company commander was a veteran of World War II who had decided that the postwar army would make a secure, comfortable career. However, the fighting in Korea was more than he bargained for.

He stood up and started his presentation. "Gentlemen, here is the plan. The cooks will start serving breakfast at 0730. The company will load up and prepare to start moving north as soon as the Marines vacate their positions. The mission is to attack north in pursuit of the North Korean forces. According to the Marines, there are no enemy units in the immediate vicinity. Be sure and keep a close watch on your men for signs of frostbite. If we keep the gooks on the run for a few more days, maybe we can wrap this campaign up. Does anyone have any questions?"

"What about the chinks, Captain?" the young leader of the First Platoon asked.

"The Marines seem to think that there are only a few of them and that they are not in this area. It was reported that some were sighted off to the northeast near the Chosin Reservoir and that the Intelligence and Reconnaissance Platoon (I & R) was going over to scout it out. Any other questions? That's it then, gentlemen. If anyone would like to check the map and get a better idea of the situation, feel free to do so," the company commander stated.

Second Lieutenant John Schneidermann moved over to the map board lying on the table. The rectangular plywood board had a transparent mylar cover taped to the board on three sides. A topographic map had been placed under the plastic, and various symbols had been drawn on the mylar cover with grease pencils. The platoon leader studied the map board, observing the terrain features and the locations of the different units.

To the west were the various elements of the 1st Marine Division. Their forward headquarters and supply base were at the town of Hagru-ri near the south end of the Chosin Reservoir. To the left of the reservoir were symbols indicating the 5th and 7th marine regiments poised to advance to the village of Yudan-ni. On the east side of the Chosin was a single road winding along the shore and through the hills in a north-south direction. The 5th Marines had been originally ordered to advance along the east side but were now being replaced by the army troops of the 7th Infantry Division. Shown on the map were these units of the improvised Regimental Combat Team designated as the 31st RCT. There in black grease pencil was an impersonal series of symbols representing about 3000 infantry and artillery soldiers, each an individual with his own hopes and fears, successes, and failures.

| | | | | |
|---|---|---|---|---|
| ⊠ | 1st Bn, 32nd Inf, | | ⊠ | 3rd Bn, 31st Inf, |
| ▣ | HM Co, 31st Inf, | | ⧄ | Tk Co, 31st Inf, |
| ⊡ | HQ Co, 31st Inf, | | ▢ | Ser Co, 31st Inf, |
| ⊞ | Med Co, 31st Inf, | | ▣ | 57th FA Bn (-), |
| ᴀᴀ | Bat D, 15th AAA | | | |

Second Lieutenant John W. Schneidermann left the company CP, slowly picking his way back to the platoon area. Although he had only been in the company for a few short days, it seemed as if he had known nothing else. Life in the infantry was another world, a world of the basics: fatigue and rest, order and confusion, danger and safety. It was an unreal world, almost like a movie scene come to life on the cold, bleak, Asian landscape. Events had been moving at a fast pace, and now who knows what will happen next. The lieutenant thought: *One thing about rapidly moving action is that it doesn't give you much time to think. Probably just as well.*

The 7th Infantry Division had been in action since landing on the East Coast of Korea at Inchon about two months previously. The 7th Infantry Division had backed up the 1st Marine Division, the unit that successfully accomplished the amphibious operation. The two divisions that formed the X Corps then went on to capture Seoul, the South Korean capital. These actions, together with a determined defense of the Pusan perimeter, broke the back of the North Korean military. The NKA had hoped for a quick, decisive thrust that would make them masters of the peninsula. Now the NKA was in full retreat, and it looked like the campaign was all but over. The only dark clouds on the horizon were China or the Soviet Union. Second Lieutenant John Schneidermann raised the flap of the canvas door to the CP bunker. The two sergeants were squatting around the pocket stove. There was a certain cozy atmosphere in the sturdy emplacement. Referring to the written comments in his notebook, he repeated the general plan of action. The platoon sergeant spoke up. "I'll coordinate the breakfast schedule with the first sergeant if that's OK with you, Lieutenant."

"Sounds good, Sergeant. Another thing. I'll have a father and son talk with the squad leaders about last night's guard fiasco. Polowski, roll out. Tell the squad leaders that I want to see them right away." The runner slowly rolled over in his sleeping bag, groping for the zipper.

Second Lieutenant John Schneidermann addressed the platoon sergeant, "I'll go over and check out our trucks."

"OK, Sir."

The bivouac area was beginning to stir. Numerous fires were starting to break the pre-dawn darkness. The old saying, "It's always darkest before dawn," is apparent to the field soldier. The wind had died down, but the cold was still stalking the dark landscape. The men of the company were crawling out of the positions that they had occupied during the night. At the different campfires, a circle of disheveled, groggy soldiers gathered to soak up the warmth.

The mess tent bustled with activity. The cooks and their helpers had several gas-fired, field ranges going full blast. Large aluminum containers of hot coffee gave off a delicious aroma. Several grills were heating over the ranges. A scattering of men was convening in the mess area. The mess personnel had formed a serving line and were doling out a hot breakfast: pancakes, fried bacon, coffee, and sliced peaches. Not a bad meal, even under the circumstances.

"Would you care for some chow, Lieutenant?"

"Not right now, thanks." John Schneidermann believed in the rule that your men come first. Not every officer did. The mess tent formed a center of life--a link to the unit and home and a promise of better things ahead.

Streaks of light were now forming over the hills to the east. The cold seemed to be less intense. The forms of men, vehicles, and tents were now taking shape. The outline of all the familiar figures began emerging from the grip of the darkness.

A row of trucks was parked along the edge of the narrow dirt track. Second Lieutenant John Schneidermann, son of the Northern Plains and lover of vehicles and farm machinery, walked along the line of the dusty trucks.

These trucks, the familiar 6x6s, were the mainstay of the army. They gave the impression of ruggedness with their solid construction and utilitarian features: heavy bumpers, tow hooks, solid cabs with no tops or heaters, and canvas-covered bodies. The lieutenant, from force of habit, mentally checked the units just as the prairie farmers checked their machinery. He walked slowly up one side and down the other. After bending down by one wheel, the lieutenant quickly straightened up and started toward the company kitchen, where a line of men stood in front of the serving tables with mess kits in hand.

"Is the driver of Service 12 around here?" the lieutenant questioned.

"That's me, Lieutenant," came a voice from the group.

"I'd like to see you for a minute."

From the line of men waiting to be served, a slight, thin-faced young soldier emerged. The driver had an unkempt appearance with a dirty, unbuttoned parka, unlaced boots, and a beginning beard. "What is it, Lieutenant?"

"I was looking at your truck, and I noticed that there is one missing wheel nut and three loose ones on the right front wheel."

The driver swallowed with a surprised gulp. This was not your usual young infantry second lieutenant looking at him with a steady, calm gaze. "That's great. Do you have a wheel wrench?"

"Yes, there's one in the truck, and I think I can find a wheel nut, too."

Second Lieutenant John Schneidermann walked back to the platoon area. A fire was going near the CP, and the men of the platoon were moving back and forth, getting ready for a new day. One squad was moving off in single file toward the mess tent. Packs were rolled and lined up by squads. The machine guns were set up on their tripods side by side, with their boxes of ammunition neatly stacked by each gun.

The platoon sergeant had things moving smoothly, as was his usual forte. Men were moving with purpose in their steps. The daylight was becoming brighter as the tempo of activity picked up. The platoon was getting ready for their motor march to the north.

"How is it going?" Sergeant Pratt platoon leader queried.

"Everything is on track, Sir. The men will draw C-Rations for the next two meals."

"Looks good, Sergeant," the lieutenant commented.

The platoon sergeant continued, "I talked to the squad leaders about last night's guard problem. The gooks have a method of dealing with sleeping guards. They make up the judge, the jury, and the executioner. The sentence is a bayonet between the ribs."

When the squad leaders arrived at the CP, the runner and the medic immediately vacated the area. The platoon sergeant directed the four men to sit as he silently stood with a serious expression on his face. "This is going to be short. Last night the lieutenant checked the line and found four men awake when there should have been eight. The machine guns had two men on guard, so what I am saying won't apply to you, Sergeant Cobb. In one squad, everyone was asleep; in the other two rifle squads, one man was awake. Does anyone have anything to say?" Total silence. "This is not going to happen again." The sergeant raised his voice. "If I ever find anyone asleep on guard, there won't be a court-martial; they won't be reported to the company commander; the lieutenant won't be involved, and do you know why?" There was an uncomfortable silence. Sergeant Pratt paced as he talked. A well-built individual, at that moment he looked formidable. It was well known that he was quick with his fists. It was rumored around the company that an individual who had crossed the sergeant had been severely beaten. The sergeant was looking pugnacious at the moment. He seemed to become more menacing as he spoke. "If no one knows why, I'll tell you why." The four men were avoiding the sergeant's direct gaze. "The reason is I am going to personally beat the crap out of anyone I find sleeping on guard. If anyone wants to call me, now is the time to speak up." No one moved or spoke. "Now, do you men understand what I am talking about?" The four men quietly nodded. "If there is nothing further, that is all."

The platoon was typical. While a full-strength rifle platoon is about forty men, it had about thirty-four men and one officer. Included in this number were thirteen ROK soldiers, young men who had been pressed into service with little or no training. Between the ROKs and their US counterparts was a wide cultural gap. The ROKs were improving, but it was taking time. A rifle platoon is an intimate group like a football team where each member knows all the other members. Like any team, success depends on several factors: the skill of the individuals, the leadership ability of the officers and non-coms, the availability of supporting weapons, an adequate supply situation, and a certain amount of old-fashioned luck. Second Lieutenant John W. Schneiderman's platoon, typical of the rifle platoons of the 7th Infantry Division, had several weak areas.

The morale of the men of the platoon was high despite the cold, the desolation, and harsh living conditions. The end was in sight, and most importantly, they were winning. A certain element of high exuberance comes with winning in infantry combat. The initial dread of injury, death, and the unknown gives way to way to a wild sense of an overpowering mastery of life. Nothing is quite like seeing a beaten enemy running and then firing a few shots to speed them on their way. At that point, the infantry soldier feels ten feet tall and that he can lick the world.

The last squad was now moving toward the mess area in eager anticipation of a substantial hot breakfast. The mess kits jingled as the men walked along. The platoon leader and his second-in-command followed at the rear of the squad. The mess tent was still bustling with activity. The delicious aroma of frying bacon and steaming coffee drifted from the kitchen. The scene was presided over by the mess sergeant. In the army, a capable mess sergeant was truly a "pearl of great price." Most of the good ones had some major character flaw that tended to cloud their standing with the hierarchy of the company. The lieutenant and his platoon sergeant followed the last of their men through the serving line. There were trays for the two, as was the custom in the company. In most units of the Regular Army, certain courtesies were extended to the officers and senior non-coms. A hearty breakfast always went a long way toward raising the soldiers' sense of well-being.

At the end of the serving line was a box of C-Rations. Each man was given four cans which represented two meals. A C-Ration meal consisted of two cans about three inches high and three inches in diameter. One can, a dry ration, contained disc-shaped crackers, cocoa, jelly in a separate small can, and other sundry items. The other can, called the wet ration, contained one of a variety of prepared foods such as corned beef hash, ham and lima beans, or pork and beans. In very cold weather, the wet cans could freeze, which presented an unappetizing meal. If fire was available, the cans could be heated. The experienced trooper would heat the ration in boiling water. Heating the can over an open flame would usually result in a cold top half and a burned bottom half. When traveling by truck, some of the more innovative souls would heat their main dish by tying the ration to the engine manifold.

The scene around the bivouac area again changed. All the tents were down, and the trucks were in the process of loading. The rifle platoons remained close to their defensive positions because there was always the possibility of attack, even though the command considered it remote. All pointed north, the trucks moved into position along the road. Some of the trucks wouldn't start because of the extreme cold and required a boost from another vehicle. The command jeeps with their whip antennas ranged back and forth along the column like sheepdogs moving the flock into position.

Three trucks carried the platoon and its equipment, plus several members of the weapons platoon. The platoon leader rode the cab of the first truck, the assistant platoon sergeant, the second, and the platoon sergeant, the third. At last, the truck column, which was made up of the entire battalion, was ready to move north. All morning a stream of dusty trucks and jeeps of the 5th Marine Regiment were heading south. It was apparent that the battalion would be moving up to occupy their vacated positions.

The men of the Marine Regiments were impressive specimens. They moved with an air of confidence and elan. This was no doubt due to their excellent physical condition and the fact that there were many veterans of the Pacific battles of World War II.

The army battalion waited as the Marine column continued to roll south. The narrow road made it impossible for the two columns to move simultaneously. Except for a few single jeeps, the flow of vehicles was to the south.

There is something inspiring about an army on the move--a sense of history and adventure. The spirit of the old army, of "40 miles a day on beans and hay," seemed to be a part of the long, drab column of trucks and jeeps. The men congregated on the leeward side of the vehicles keeping circulation going by stamping their feet and clapping their hands. The usual horseplay among the troops signaled that the morale of the men was reasonably high.

No evidence of any enemy activity had been observed by any member of the battalion. The silent hills seemed barren and empty of life. No shots had been heard, and no dark figures on the distant skyline.

Second Lieutenant John Schneidermann, the prairie farmer, ordered the drivers to check their engine oil.

"Hey, Lieutenant, it isn't necessary do all this checking," the drivers protested, but the platoon leader held firm, standing by while each hood was opened and the oil levels verified.

The men of the platoon were young, most under 21. With youth there is a spirit of optimism, spontaneity, and of immortality. Among them was the usual compliment of characters: tellers of tales, the chronic hypochondriacs, the gripers, loners, and intellectuals. Some were highly intelligent, some average, and some not too bright. A wide variety of skills and occupations was represented: students, farmers, auto mechanics, truck drivers, store clerks, and salesmen. Now they were riflemen, gunners, and scouts—a fair collections of fighters. The men were gathered in small groups, some smoking, others engaged in conversation, some silently listening, while others were just content to lean against a vehicle. The strains of "Waltzing Matilda" on the harmonica drifted over the platoon. The harmonica was a true infantryman's musical instrument--compact, and not too difficult to play.

Second Lieutenant John Schneidermann and Sergeant Pratt were using the time to meet with the individual squad leaders. One at a time, they walked to the lead truck, where they would look for any problems.

"Any big problems?" the platoon leader asked as an opener.

The squad leader replied, "The main rub is these damn ROKs. I don't think they're ever going to make soldiers. They don't know their weapons. They don't know what they're supposed to do. You know, the basic things that everybody should know. Other than that, everything is OK. But it would be nice to get some more to eat, especially some candy bars. In this cold weather, C-Rations just don't give you enough energy." The young squad leader was a serious twenty-year-old. The changes he recommended were real, and he was totally sincere in making them.

An infantry squad leader is a key man in any army. It's true to say that an army is no better than its squad leaders. In the heat of battle, when the forces have been committed, when all the carefully laid plans have been shattered, and when all communications are out, it is the small unit leaders that win the day. It is neither the high commanders nor the political leaders that the forward rifleman is thinking about but his squad leader. This is the leader he can see and hear, a man who can lead by example. And when that last bit of effort is made, the effort that wins the battle, it is the squad leader that is there fanning that faint spark of determination. Thus, it is essential that the squad leaders be recognized for what they are--the essential factor of success. If you want a good army, develop good squad leaders.

The platoon sergeant replied to the young squad leader, "Those are important comments. We will keep them in mind. Be sure that you keep checking your men for frostbite. Make foot inspections. Check the weapons to make sure they work. You do much fighting with a weapon that won't fire."

# Moving North

Toward noon the order came down that the battalion would be moving in the early afternoon. The men began to build cooking fires with what available fuel could be found. Soon an assortment of containers was in the fires, steaming with boiling water. The men of the platoon gathered around the fires heating their rations and soaking up any available heat. Always a certain amount of trading transpired. A ham and lima bean for a corn beef hash, cigarettes for cocoa.

Finally, after the last element of the Marine column had passed out of sight to the south, the battalion began moving up the road to the north. The trucks moved at a slow, deliberate pace, the many wheels churning up dust as they rolled along. The single-lane dirt road climbed over a saddle east of the peak of Hill 1221. From there, it angled west, crossed a bridge over an inlet stream, and then followed the edge of the reservoir and a narrow-gage railroad for several miles. The road then crossed another bridge, switched to the west along a bay of the reservoir, and then turned sharply north. In about two miles, the battalion came to the positions recently abandoned by the Marines. When the convoy pulled to a stop along the side of the road, the men climbed slowly down the tailgates and assembled beside the trucks. The platoon moved off toward their assigned positions in single file. They had to travel on foot for about a quarter of a mile.

Because the section of line to be occupied by the platoon had been well constructed by the previous occupants, no work was necessary. It was a "good deal" to be able to climb into existing trenches, holes, and bunkers that were there for the taking. The platoon leader walked the line checking each squad position.

"This isn't bad at all, Lieutenant, to inherit these nice diggings," remarked a cheerful rifleman. "Too bad we can't stay here longer than one night."

The platoon sergeant had located a roomy, well-built bunker just to the rear of the platoon line. He proceeded to set up housekeeping and establish communication with the company CP. The runner, the medic, and the assistant platoon sergeant also occupied the bunker. The men started small fires in some of the unused holes and began heating water. It was a satisfactory day, a short motor march, a move into prepared positions, time to set up a defensive line, and time for a leisurely supper. The morale in the platoon was high, as was usually the case of a unit moving forward, always with hope for a better tomorrow and the thought that the enemy was on the run.

After checking his line and making sure that the fields of defensive fire looked proper, the platoon leader walked toward the new CP. The temperature was falling as darkness approached. The lieutenant ducked into the CP bunker. The interior was cozy with the soft light from a burning candle and the smell of food. There were convenient shelves made from wooden ammunition boxes and hooks to store equipment on. An old shelter half formed a door to the single entrance. The lieutenant was greeted in a hearty manner. "Come on in, we got us the first-class hooch," the platoon sergeant called out. "We heated some rations and saved you one."

"Thanks, Sergeant. I could use a hot can of beans about now."

The five men relaxed around the interior of the bunker. "How come you stayed in the army, Sergeant Pratt?" the runner queried.

"Well, it was like this, Polowski. When it came time to re-enlist, it was always winter, and the garbage cans were frozen over."

"How's the army been treating you, Lieutenant? Is soldiering better than being a Minnesota farmer?" The platoon sergeant inquired, grinning.

"So far, so good. If it doesn't get any worse than this, I think I'll make it."

For some minutes, all was silent except for the flapping of the canvas and the low sputtering of the candle. It was one of those pleasant times a soldier remembers.

The platoon sergeant finally broke the silence. "I guess we better get the guard schedule set up. What time would you prefer, Lieutenant?"

"I'll take the second shift if that's OK."

"All right. The lieutenant will take the 2200 to 2400 slot. Garza, you take the 2000-to-2200-hour shift. Ridehout, you take the 2400 to 0200 slot. Polowski, you pull the 0200 to 0400 shift. I'll take 0400 to morning".

The platoon leader rose to a half-standing position. "I'll check the line one more time and then catch a little shut-eye, Sergeant."

"OK, Lieutenant. We'll see you later."

27

# Setting the Stage

And so it was that on the night of Monday, the 27th of November, the improvised 31st Infantry Regimental Combat Team was camped along the east shore of the Chosin Reservoir. About three thousand strong, the RCT was commanded by Colonel Allan D. MacLean, CO of the 31st Infantry Regiment.

The Units of the 31st RCT were positioned at several major locations along the single lane, dirt road that wound along the east shore of the reservoir. The most northerly element was the 1st Battalion, 32nd Infantry, located about twelve miles north of Hagaru-ri, the location of the advanced headquarters of the 1st Marine Division. About a half mile south of the 1st Battalion, 32nd Infantry was the Heavy Mortar Company, 31st Infantry, armed with the big 4.2-inch mortars. About a quarter mile south of Heavy Mortar Company was the advanced CP of the 31st Infantry. Farther down the road and south of the causeway and bridge was a perimeter containing the 3rd Battalion, 31st Infantry, and Batteries A and B of the 57th Field Artillery Battalion. Another one-and one-half miles further down the road were HQ Battery, 57th Field Artillery Battalion, and part of Battery D, 15th AAA AW Battalion. The AAA Battery was equipped with four M-19 full-tracked units, each with twin 40 mm cannons, and four M-16 half-tracked units, each with four .50 caliber machine guns. About another four road miles south was the Tank Company, 31st Infantry, and the rear CP of the 31st Infantry. The tank company was equipped with a full complement of twenty-two M 4A4 tanks. Twenty of the tanks were armed with 76 mm cannons, and the other two had 105 mm cannons as their main armament. Another two miles down the road to the south was Service Battery, 57th Field Artillery Battalion. The stage was now set for a tragedy of major proportions for the 3000 soldiers of the 31st RCT.

Under Major General Edward M. Almond, the US X Army was driving north in an effort to totally capture the Korean Peninsula. General Almond, a protege of General Douglas MacArthur, was pressing relentlessly on with a goal of a quick advance to the Manchurian border. Winter weather was fast arriving and the terrain forbidding, but with victory in sight, the order was to advance without delay. General MacArthur had won a spectacular victory at Inchon, winning despite great reservations by many knowledgeable and experienced commanders of all the services. Considering this triumph, General MacArthur's plan to "end the war by Christmas" did not seem unreasonable. The unknown factor was the Chinese forces which General MacArthur and his subordinate commanders failed to fully take into consideration. About a month earlier, Chinese combat forces had suddenly appeared on the west side of the peninsula and attacked units of the US Eighth Army. They had shaken the American and ROK forces and then pulled back. Now other Chinese units were poised to strike again. As the men of the 31st RCT were in position on the night of November 27, expecting to resume their advance in the morning, the patient, disciplined, hardy soldiers of the Peoples' Liberation Army launched a massive infantry assault on the unsuspecting US troops.

The temperature was definitely dropping. The cold had a way of reaching through clothing, no matter how thick or well-insulated. Second Lieutenant John W. Schneidermann stood outside the bunker and searched the area with an inquiring gaze. The sky was overcast, and light snow was in the air. The nearest portion of the platoon line was clearly visible. The shapes of the riflemen made dark outlines against the white snow.

In a few steps, the platoon leader reached the nearest position. Three men of the squad occupied a short section of the trench which was connected to a small bunker. The rifle squad leader was one of the three men in the emplacement.

"How's it going, Sergeant?" the platoon leader inquired.

"Everything's quiet, Sir."

"Good. Keep on the alert."

The lieutenant walked the length of the line, stopping to visit with each of the four squad leaders. At the weapons squad, he crawled down behind each of the two light .30 caliber machine guns. The guns were set up to work as a team. When one gun stops reloading, the other will continue firing. In that way, the field of fire would always be covered.

"How many boxes do you have for each gun?" the platoon leader wanted to know.

The squad leader, a young native of Alabama, replied, "Six boxes for each gun is the basic load, but we got ten boxes, Suh… That's at least 2500 rounds."

"Are the guns ready to fire, Sergeant? "

"Yes, Sir. These guns are in good shape. We check the guns every day and clean them whenever they look like they need cleaning. We test-fired them just before coming up here."

"We got a spare barrel in this here case, and we got a headspace gage," the squad leader reported.

"Looks good, Sergeant. Stay alert." Second Lieutenant John W. Schneidermann slowly and carefully walked back to the platoon CP. The terrain features now began to show up in greater detail: the trenches, bunkers, rocks, and trees. The young officer thought: *It seems unreal to be here in this bleak corner of a distant Asian country, a wilderness of cold, mountains, and snow. Maybe in the morning, when the attack gets going, things will get back to reality--if we can just make it to the Yalu and win the war or police action or whatever it is. But life hasn't been too bad--the men in the platoon have been pretty patient with a greenhorn "shave tail" who hasn't seen a live enemy and may never see one. After all, these guys made the Inchon landing and captured Seoul, which was no small fight. Maybe if there is some combat, I won't make the grade, chicken out, or freeze. It has happened to other people.*

The lieutenant ducked through the canvas door of the CP. The platoon sergeant was sitting on an old wooden ammunition box, looking relaxed and at peace with the world. "What time have you got, Lieutenant?"

"I show 2030 on my watch," the platoon leader replied. "If you want to get a little sleep, go ahead. I'll stay up until 2200."

"That sounds good to me, Sergeant. I checked the line, and everything is looking good. I think your talk with the squad leaders really paid off."

"I hope so, Sir. You have to keep on those guys because if you don't, they get sloppy. I chewed 'em out pretty good."

The sleeping forms of the medic, the runner, and the assistant platoon sergeant lay against the walls of the bunker. The platoon leader crawled into his mummy bag and pulled up the zipper. He drifted off to sleep within a few minutes--a true infantryman can sleep anywhere. Sleep is a precious commodity to the field soldier going back to the dawn of time when men fought with spears and clubs.

# Morning

"Get up, John. It's time to get rolling." John Schneidermann sat up as his dad lightly shook his shoulder.

"OK, I'm coming." John swung his feet out and began pulling on his clothes. Long underwear, then a heavy flannel shirt, a pair of well-worn jeans with red suspenders, boot socks, a pair of moccasin-type hunting boots, an insulated vest, and a thick sweatshirt with a hood completed the outfit, typical garb for the prairie farmer. A seed corn cap and a leather holster with a pair of pliers were also part of the kit. Yellow cloth gloves and low pull-on overshoes were at the back door.

The savory aroma of breakfast drifted up to meet him as John Schneidermann tripped down the stairway. On the kitchen table, prepared by Mrs. Schneidermann, was a typical Midwest farm breakfast of bacon, fried eggs, toast, homemade jelly, coffee, and juice. The young farmer sat up to the table and began filling his plate.

"Well, John, we've can keep rolling, we'll finish up the north place," his dad stated.

"Yeah, if the old picker holds together. You know, Dad, we really ought to think about getting a new one. I think I've fixed every chain on that thing."

You might be right, son. Maybe after the corn is in and we have some time, we'll look into it."

After breakfast, John Schneidermann and his father abruptly got up from the table, picked up their black lunch buckets, and headed out the back door of the farmhouse and into the black night. The battered pickup truck was covered with a light coating of frost. John found a scraper in the glove compartment and scraped off the windows of the light truck. The two men climbed into the cab and started the engine of the pickup. In a few short minutes, the truck started down the driveway.

# Without Warning

"2200 hours, Lieutenant." The platoon sergeant lightly shook the platoon leader by the shoulder.

Second Lieutenant John W. Schneidermann sat up and unzipped the sleeping bag. "I sure hate to get out of a sleeping bag." He untangled his lanky frame from the warm folds of the down-filled bag. Like most soldiers, he had taken off his boots and jacket before getting in. "Man, I sure slept like a rock. Anything going on, Sergeant?"

"Not much. I've been calling the company every half hour. Not much action with the other companies either."

The platoon leader checked his .45 caliber pistol. It was a Colt government model, which he carried in a shoulder holster under his field jacket. "I could use a little more sleep, but duty calls, right, Sergeant?"

The platoon sergeant appeared to be in no hurry to sleep. He slowly pulled off his overshoes and carefully unbuttoned his field jacket. After several minutes he slipped into his sleeping bag. The interior of the bunker, while relatively neat, was still cluttered with the usual collection of equipment, weapons, and ammunition. The lieutenant thought, "In some ways, cold weather is better than warmer, rainy conditions. At least the bunkers are dry. Cold may be good, but not this cold.

The platoon leader called the company CP on the sound-powered phone and reported in. "Negative here." The sweep hands on the army issue watch seemed to move like a living thing marking the passage of time. The other four men were asleep--each making distinct sounds. The flickering light from the candle threw shadows on the exposed dirt walls of the bunker. Suddenly, a series of rifle shots broke the stillness of the black night. The shooting continued for several minutes. The platoon leader picked up the phone, "3rd Platoon on. What's the shooting all about?"

The company headquarters operator replied, "Don't know yet, Lieutenant. Might be the ROKs."

The firing went on sporadically, seeming to come from the right of the platoon positions. After about twenty minutes, the lieutenant roused the platoon sergeant. "There's been firing for a while now. I'm going to check the line. "Maybe you could cover the phone."

"OK, Lieutenant. I'll hold the fort."

Second Lieutenant John W. Schneidermann grabbed his rifle from a peg on the wall, picked up two bandoliers of ammunition, and ducked out the bunker's canvas door. The cold air hit his face like a blast from the Arctic. The platoon leader sucked in his breath and began a visual search of the ground to his front. On the right, further down the line, rifle fire was popping in the night air. Occasionally a flash could be seen. The lieutenant stood in the trench, observing, his night vision slowly developing. Without warning, several rifles opened fire on the platoon line immediately forward of the CP. The platoon leader moved stealthily to the nearest squad position. The three men in the position were all awake and on their feet. The lieutenant scrambled to the trench and jumped in beside the squad leader. "What's going on, Sergeant?"

The sergeant was a stocky young man, a native of New York City, swarthy, with a shock of black hair. "There's something out there, sir," the squad leader replied.

"What do you think it is?" the platoon leader asked.

"I saw something moving right to our front," the sergeant continued.

"Were you firing?"

"No, it came from farther to the left." For several minutes the four men stood stock still, listening intently. An occasional shot cracked from both left and right. After about a half hour, the firing stopped altogether. Only the sighing of the wind broke the silence.

The lieutenant leaned over to the squad leader. "I'm going back to the CP, DiAngelo."

"OK, Lieutenant. We'll stay on top of it here."

The platoon leader stepped carefully down the dim path to the platoon CP.

Back at the platoon CP, the platoon sergeant was sitting up, half out of his sleeping bag. He looked up as the lieutenant slid through the doorway. "What's happening up there, Sir?"

"It's hard to tell. DiAngelo says that he saw something moving in front of the line," the platoon leader replied. "I called the company, and they say that there've been several reports of movement to the front of the line."

"What do you think is going on, Sergeant?" the lieutenant queried.

"I just don't know, Lieutenant. Maybe it's some rear-guard effort by the North Koreans. We better get these guys up and on alert at the CP," spoke the platoon sergeant in a serious tone. He began rousing the slumbering men of the headquarters group. "Let's go, you guys. Up and at 'em," the sergeant called. The three men reluctantly sat up, yawning, and rubbing their eyes. The platoon sergeant issued a crisp order, "We better have somebody outside in the trench; there's been a lot of shooting, and we don't know what's going on. Polowski, you take the first shift." In a flurry of activity, the men rolled out of their sleeping gear and made ready for action.

Sometime after midnight, 2400 hours, some scattered shots came again from somewhere beyond the infantry line. Second Lieutenant John Schneidermann turned and, in a few short bounds, made it to the first squad position. The squad leader was awake and on his feet in the fighting trench. The platoon leader landed beside him with a leap.

"What do you see, Sergeant?" the lieutenant asked in a low whisper.

"Nothing, Sir. Those shots came from the left," the squad leader answered. The two men continued to peer into the black night.

Suddenly, total chaos descended on the infantry line. A tremendous volume of firing instantly broke out. The platoon leader pulled his rifle from his shoulder and brought it to a firing position. Some mortar rounds began falling somewhere to the rear of the platoon position. The lieutenant shouted an order, "Check the rest of the squad and make sure everyone is up and ready."

The shadows to the front began to move--silent forms, changing shapes, dodging, weaving like a running back running going for a touchdown. Second Lieutenant John W. Schneidermann took hasty aim and fired. A shadow disappeared, and others kept moving--forward, sideways, backward. The platoon began firing in earnest. The sounds of bugle calls floated over the snow-covered fighting line. Form a sight picture and squeeze the trigger. Shift to another target, a moving shadow figure silently gliding toward the rifle squad position. Squeeze the trigger. Repeat the process. The clip made a distinct "ping" as it popped from the receiver. Find an eight-round clip, push it down into the open receiver, and slam the bolt shut. Sight on a moving target, squeeze the trigger again and again. Repeat the movements. Find a clip, load the rifle, find a target, and squeeze the trigger, again and again. From both left and right, the sounds of firing continued, rising in volume. The distinct chatter of the light machine guns and the short bursts of the automatic rifles could be heard. Smoke floated across the firing line. Mortar rounds were exploding to the front of the platoon. A flare lighted the scene, and the shadow figures became, for a moment, a man in padded clothes, moving ever forward. The M-1 rifle in the hand of the platoon leader was working

34

without any hint of a malfunction. The sequence of loading and firing was now automatic, total reflex, no thought process at all. Out of the hot rifle, the sound and smell of grease cooking were noticeable.

Rage was building in the platoon leader--the blood of the Viking warrior, the crusader, the medieval soldier long dormant now rose to the surface. Only one goal--kill the shadow figures that had dared to challenge the ancient fighters.

Heavy mortars were firing somewhere to the rear, dropping shells forward of the firing line, adding to the symphony of battle. The young lieutenant from the northern plains was now locked in a single mission, totally oblivious to all other influences. The repetition of sighting on the target, squeezing the trigger, and reloading continued without a pause or break in the rhythm. A sequence of motions learned over years of practice had taken control of his thought process.

The shadow figures began fading away. The deadly fire from the single rifle had softened their impact. Many of the padded bodies lay still, scattered at random in grotesque tangles. The rushing tide receded and melted away. Second Lieutenant John W. Schneidermann stopped firing. No more targets were in sight. He began to return from the scenes of ancient conflicts, of clashing steel, of smoke, and fire. The images of the present came into focus.

The squad leader, DiAngelo, was breathing heavily. "You sure gave them hell, Lieutenant. I have never seen anybody shoot an M-1 rifle like that!"

The platoon leader turned and eyed the sergeant with a quizzical stare. A sense of command responsibility began to penetrate the lieutenant's thought process. Now a need for immediate action was pressing on the young officer. He gave a brief order: "Check your squad, Sergeant, and report back." The platoon leader then moved to the left at a low crouch. He called out in a loud whisper as he approached the next squad position. "This is Lieutenant Schneidermann. Are you OK?"

The squad leader, O'Malley, replied, "We're hanging in there. One man hit."

Keeping low to stay out of the line of fire, the lieutenant moved along the infantry line. "Can the man get back to the aid station on his own?" the lieutenant asked.

"Sure. Only a nick," the squad leader answered.

"If it's not too bad, maybe he better stay here until it gets light. We'll try to get the medic up here as soon as possible."

The next squad was the machine gun position. "How are you doing, Sergeant?"

"One man didn't make it, Suh, and two more are hit."

The lieutenant moved over to where the squad leader sat beside the light .30 caliber gun. The gun had been firing, as evidenced by the pile of expended metal belt links and cartridges that had formed under the gun.

At one end of the short trench, an individual in bulky clothes was leaning against the wall of the emplacement. He appeared to be asleep but was, in reality, dead. "What happened, Sergeant?" the lieutenant asked.

"We saw a lot of movement directly to our front and began firing with one gun. They started rushing us, and we really opened up. That's when Anderson got it. It must have been a bullet because they never got too close. Two of the ROKs were hit at about the same time. I don't think they are going to make it," the squad leader answered in a slow, deliberate monotone.

"How is your ammunition supply?" the lieutenant asked.

"We're in pretty good shape, Suh. We got at least six boxes left for each gun."

"You did one hell of a job, Sergeant Cobb. Hang in there. Try to get the wounded back to the aid station, if at all possible." The platoon leader spoke in a low, steady voice.

"Thank you, Suh."

The platoon leader threaded his way back to the platoon CP. The snow was coming down in intermittent showers, and the wind was picking up. While the rifles along the platoon line were still firing, the volume was decreasing. Rounds from the supporting mortars were still arcing overhead, landing forward of the platoon line.

The platoon sergeant was standing in the trench adjacent to the CP bunker with his rifle at the ready. "Good to see you, Lieutenant. Is the line holding OK?"

"We're in fairly good shape, but it was one hell of an attack," the lieutenant replied. "Garza, better get up to the line right away. Two men in the fourth squad are hurt bad," he stated in a firm, steady voice.

The medic emerged from the bunker just as the platoon leader was speaking. "I'll get up there right away, Sir," the medic quietly stated as he left the trench with his medical kit in hand.

The platoon leader ducked into the bunker and reached for the phone. The first sergeant responded to his whistle. "This is Schneidermann. We are holding in good order; we have one KIA and three WIA that I know of."

"Listen, Lieutenant, hell is breaking out all over. We are being attacked along the whole battalion perimeter. Hold on 'til daylight if you possibly can."

Second Lieutenant John W. Schneidermann leaned against the wall of the bunker as if to grasp a piece of reality. It was dawning on the men of the battalion that this was no half-hearted delaying action by a beaten enemy. This was an all-out attack by a powerful foe whose objective was the destruction of the U.S. forces. The men of the platoon were holding well after the sudden initial assault. Now the mission was to keep holding until dawn when the superior supporting weapons of the Americans could be brought to bear.

The young officer's whole being was shaking from the unbelievable events of the night. He thought: *Can this really be happening? What is going to take place now? Get hold of yourself. A whole platoon of men needs a leader, and they need one bad.* An overpowering sense of isolation typical in infantry combat was present here, this acute feeling of being alone, the last outpost of the last company of the last battalion.

There was a pressing need for action in the mind of the platoon leader. He turned to the platoon sergeant, "You and Polowski stay in the CP. I'll take Ridehout with me and we'll go up to the line. Stay in close contact with the company. It would be great if we could get a forward observer up here, but I suppose that's not possible." The platoon leader and the assistant platoon sergeant each picked up a dozen bandoliers and slung them over their shoulders. They moved out into the darkness toward the firing line.

The squad leader, DiAngelo, was in his trench along with two other members of the squad. "What's up, Sergeant?" the platoon leader asked in a low voice.

"Things have quieted down. We haven't seen any movement lately," the sergeant replied.

The lieutenant asked, "How's your ammunition holding out?"

"Each rifleman has about 100 rounds, and the ARs are back up to their 400 rounds. I had them reload all the magazines," the squad leader answered.

Second Lieutenant John W. Schneidermann gave a brisk order to the assistant platoon sergeant, "Crawl over to the right flank squad and see how they are doing."

He immediately started to the right in a low crouch. The platoon leader and Sergeant DiAngelo, the squad leader, kept staring into the night, both straining for any sign of renewed enemy action.

"Maybe they're giving up the attack, Lieutenant," the squad leader commented.

"Could be. One of the guys thought he saw something about fifteen minutes ago out near that clump of brush," the squad leader whispered quietly. Both men continued to peer intently into the shifting pattern of blowing snow.

"That could be an avenue of attack. There's a small draw just behind that brush," the lieutenant observed.

The sounds of battle from the rest of the battalion perimeter could still be heard, rising and falling like the low notes of a concert orchestra. The snow and wind had the effect of distorting sound both in volume and direction. It was all part of the drama that was played out in this remote mountainous region of the Korean Peninsula.

Sergeant Ridehout returned from the right flank of the platoon line, moving low, trying to keep out of the line of fire. "That squad is just fine, Sir. They haven't done any firing; they said that they just didn't see anything to shoot at," the sergeant reported.

After a certain length of time, and it was difficult to measure time in the battle situation, a slight movement appeared at the front of the squad position. Sergeant DiAngelo was the first to notice it. He tugged on the lieutenant's sleeve and, in a whisper, spoke, "Do you see that?"

Second Lieutenant John Schneidermann stood perfectly still and strained all senses as he looked intently at the area indicated by the squad leader. Could they be massing for another attack?

The sound of many voices seemed to be coming from the suspected location. The lieutenant suddenly turned to the assistant platoon sergeant, "Sergeant Ridehout, go back to the CP and see if you can contact the 81s and get them to fire to our front. Check the map and give them the coordinates of the suspected target. Report back as soon as they shoot, and we will try to adjust their fire."

The assistant platoon sergeant immediately jumped from the trench, dashing for the CP as the men on the line continued to observe their front.

The lieutenant removed his binoculars from their brown leather case and scanned the terrain with a sweeping motion. In the darkness, objects tend to become distorted. Rocks, trees, and irregularities in the ground assume suspicious shapes. Under the stress of combat, the shapes change and shift in the minds of the intent watchers. The snow continued to fall and, driven by the wind, formed a curtain over the landscape.

Second Lieutenant John W. Schneidermann continued to scan the area for suspicious enemy activity. He thought, "Is anyone really there? Maybe not. If only daylight would get here."

The sound of voices came again--a sing-song chant. This was real. Ten minutes passed… fifteen… twenty. Suddenly, without warning, there was the swish of a mortar round passing overhead. The round exploded with a flash and a bang a scant one hundred yards in front of the squad position. The shell from the 81 mm mortar fell far short of its intended target. Sergeant Ridehout appeared seconds later at the squad position. Grinning sheepishly, the assistant platoon sergeant said, "A little short, eh, Sir?"

"Yeah, go back to the phone and tell the mortars to add 200 and shift right 50."

"Yes, sir," the assistant platoon sergeant immediately dashed back to the CP, covering the twenty yards in seconds. The talking at the front appeared to get louder, floating through the darkness to the squad position. Another 81 mortar came crashing in, this time farther out and very near the target area. The platoon leader jumped from the trench and ran at top speed toward the CP bunker. Almost there, he met Sergeant Ridehout.

"Give them an add fifty and fifty right and fire for effect. Make it ten rounds if they can." The assistant platoon sergeant ducked back into the bunker; the lieutenant jogged back to the firing line. In a few short seconds, three mortar rounds landed very much on target, followed by a volley of three more rounds. After about ten seconds, a final three round volley again hit the target.

Loud cries and shouts arose from the enemy location. "I think we hit 'em, Sergeant," yelled the platoon leader. The squad leader was on his feet, jumping up and down, hollering at the top of his voice.

What was possibly an enemy force massing for another assault had apparently been disabled by the mortar barrage?

Sergeant Ridehout appeared again.

"That was great work, Sergeant. I think we took out a bunch of them," the lieutenant said with cheer.

During the next few hours, the enemy made two more attacks. They had lost their element of surprise and been hurt by the defensive fire from the 81mm mortars. The riflemen and gunners of the platoon, now thoroughly aroused, had beaten back each effort with a furious hail of rifle and machine gun fire. The platoon was performing like a team of thoroughbreds. A rifle platoon, well-entrenched and adequately supplied, was virtually invincible against an infantry attack. It was a scene reminiscent of former conflicts such as the Civil War and World War I, where massed attackers had been disastrously defeated by stubborn defenders armed with modern, long-ranged weapons.

The lieutenant and the assistant platoon sergeant stayed at their posts on the firing line. When it looked like a new assault was forming, they called for mortar fire, both high explosive and illuminating rounds. Their efficiency improved as the night wore on. The assistant platoon sergeant was getting to know the mortar platoon operators on a first-name basis.

As the first attack was in its full fury, the platoon sergeant became more and more uneasy. At last, as the attack ebbed, he made for the platoon line. He crawled the last few feet to the edge of the squad position. The picture was one of infinite confusion and conflict--the blowing snow, mortar shells swishing overhead, the crack of rifles, the high notes of bugles, smoke drifting over the firing line, the clatter of automatic weapons. The whole scene was painted on the dark background of night with the orange flashes of fire for color.

# Dawn

Daylight began to filter over the eastern hills. The scene of the battalion perimeter was one of disarray. The severe weather had not abated, adding to an already depressing picture. In the rifle platoon, the grime-covered fighters felt their spirits rise with the coming of the light. Light meant hope, for with improved visibility would come the air support that would tip the balance of power in favor of the Americans.

The air power was in the form of Marine Corsairs, black, gull-winged, propeller-driven planes that came from the carriers. The aircraft were directed by a Marine forward air controller team attached to the battalion.

Second Lieutenant John W. Schneidermann felt a surge of relief as the daylight began to strengthen. It had been the most traumatic night of his life. Now it was over. The enemy had apparently pulled back after their last assault, which had concentrated on the machine gun position. The firing had died down to only an occasional rifle shot. The top priority now was to move the wounded back to the battalion aid station and bring up rations and ammunition. It was a haggard command group that assembled outside the CP bunker. Although the temperature was rising, it was still very cold, and a light snow cover had fallen over the platoon area.

The platoon sergeant spoke out in a hoarse voice, "Ridehout, report to the company and see about getting rations and ammo up here as soon as possible. Polowski, you man the phone. Garza and I will see about getting the wounded back to the aid station." Turning to the platoon leader, he quietly said, "Sir, maybe you need a little rest. I know you had a hard night."

The platoon leader replied, "I had a rough night, all right. I think I'll check the line first. I wonder what in the hell hit us. If that was the North Korean rear guard, I'd hate to run into their main body."

The platoon sergeant spoke up, "According to the sergeant, it was the chinks. He said two were captured, and one of the ROKs talked to them. They said that they are hitting the Marines and us all at the same time."

Second Lieutenant John W. Schneidermann was tired and cold, and his muscles ached, but he was euphoric. He thought: *The chinks, eh. Well, they threw their best at us, and we licked 'em. I didn't do too bad myself. This combat business is tough, all right, but I came through with flying colors.*

41

The lieutenant made his way along the firing line stopping at each position and saying to each small group, "You did a great job, men. You held the line, and that's what counts."

The men exuded confidence as they spoke up, "What's going to happen next, Lieutenant? I hear we were up against the whole chink army. I guess we taught 'em a lesson they won't forget." The platoon leader replied, "We haven't received new orders; we'll hold here for now" To the squad leaders, he directed, "Have the men clean their weapons and wipe them dry; check each man for frostbite; rations and ammo are on the way."

The landscape changed with the arrival of daylight. The shapes were friendly now: familiar things like trees, rocks, and folds in the ground. Second Lieutenant John W. Schneidermann stopped at the squad position where he had been most of the night. He stared at the frozen land in front of the firing line. Shapes that had been living humans only a short time ago lay scattered over the ground. Silent, cloth-covered bundles, still and cold.

Squad Leader DiAngelo spoke up, breaking his thought process. "That was some great shooting, Lieutenant! Most of those stiffs out there are ones you dropped."

"Thanks, Sergeant. I'm sure you accounted for your share."

At the machine gun position, the squad leader hailed him with an air of confidence, "Good mornin', Suh. I'd like y'all to see what we bagged last night."

In front of the machine gun position lay an irregular column of bodies, all in earth-colored, padded fabric. All were lying where they fell, all killed by the deadly, efficient machine guns of the Fourth Squad. The quiet figures seemed to be struggling to advance and were now only resting, waiting to resume their forward movement. But this is no time to reflect on man's inhumanity to man. The sleeping soldiers were simply losers in the life-and-death struggle of a few short hours before.

"You showed great leadership last night, Sergeant Cobb. Without your guns, we could easily have been overrun."

"Thank you, Suh. We'll be ready again as soon as we service the guns."

The men were in high spirits despite the intensity of the night's combat. At each position were signs that the morale of the platoon was still intact--a confident grin, a thumbs up, looks of purpose. The men were shaken but had come through. The platoon spent the daylight hours resupplying, improving their positions, and picking up from the night before. The assistant platoon sergeant returned with what looked like a catered party loaded with rations and ammunition. The machine gun squad leader, not satisfied with the prescribed basic load, wandered back to the Pioneer and Ammunition Platoon and walked away with another eight boxes of belted machine gun ammunition. The platoon sergeant and the medic, Garza, had been able to move the wounded to the battalion aid station. Most of the injured could walk, but those who could not were carried on stretchers. The dead of the platoon were carried back and laid out in a row near the aid station. All along the firing line, the riflemen and gunners had settled into a relaxed stupor. They were huddling around tiny cooking fires trying to regain their composure. The men were talking back and forth, mostly about the night's action and what was going to happen in the coming hours. "They're chinks all right. I have never seen those uniforms before."

"I heard that the Colonel says we're going to start attacking as soon as the Second Battalion of the 31st gets here. We're going to be lucky to get out of here with our butts in one piece."

The platoon leader returned to the CP bunker and called the company on the phone. "Hold your position until further orders" was the word.

The runner, Polowski, was on duty at the CP. The bunker had a cluttered, lived-in look, with weapons, rations, ammunition, clothes, and equipment scattered around. The lieutenant began eating from a tin of dry rations. Halfway through a round cracker, he fell asleep sitting up. The runner threw a spare parka over the inert form.

The platoon sergeant was making the rounds of the squad positions. "You guys were on the ball last night, and I'm damn proud of you."

"What's going to happen next, Sarge?"

"We will sit tight right here until reinforcements arrive."

"How many of these here chink soldiers are we fightin', Sarge?"

"I don't know, but it doesn't matter. We'll just keep knockin' 'em down." The platoon sergeant spoke with authority, "Now get those weapons cleaned and wiped off. There's a couple of extra cleaning rods at the CP."

Second Lieutenant John W. Schneidermann slumbered on through the middle part of the 28th of November. The platoon sergeant ducked into the CP bunker. "Should I wake up the lieutenant?" asked the runner.

"Better let him sleep. He needs his rest." The platoon sergeant grinned at the slumped-over figure.

The battalion perimeter was relatively quiet during the daylight hours except for certain segments where the enemy kept up a long-range, harassing fire. At one point on the east side of the line, the Americans attempted without success to capture a high point of land. The Marine Corsairs were winging in and attacking any target of opportunity that presented itself. The Marine aircraft gave the men of the battalion much-needed support as well as raising their sense of well-being.

Shortly after 1300 hours, the platoon leader woke up with a start. For a moment, he didn't realize where he was or what had happened over the last few hours. He rubbed his eyes and looked over at the platoon runner, Polowski, who was sitting by the phone. "What time is it?" the platoon leader asked.

The platoon runner answered with a grin, "A little after noon, Sir."

The events of the night's action suddenly flooded the lieutenant's consciousness. "What's happening? Where is Sergeant Pratt?" he frantically asked.

"Everything's fine, Sir. The platoon is holding its position until further orders; Sergeant Pratt's checking the line. He said not to wake you, Sir. He said you needed the rest."

"Thanks, Polowski."

*I shouldn't be sleeping! I have responsibility for the men's welfare; that's the important thing. I better get out there and check on things* were thoughts quickly passing through the platoon leader's mind. Second Lieutenant John W. Schneidermann picked up his rifle and headed out the opening of the bunker. Although still cool, the air had warmed dramatically since the night before, but the visibility was good. Everything about the platoon seemed to be in good order. The overriding question from the men on the line was, "What's going to happen tonight?"

# Holding

The platoon leader had a standard answer: "We hold until further orders."

"I don't like the looks of this, Lieutenant. How can we fight off the whole chink army? Must have been a regiment or more that hit us last night."

"How do you like those Tommy guns they were carrying? Those Chinese were armed with U.S.-made Thompson submachine guns. It sure is a hell of a note arming your enemy with your own weapons."

The platoon sergeant was coming along the line on his way to the CP. The lieutenant called out, "Have you got a minute, Sergeant?"

"Yes, sir. Shall we meet at the CP?"

"I'll be right behind you." The two men crawled through the canvas doorway and into the interior of the bunker.

"Why don't you go over to the kitchen area and see what the plan is for supper, Polowski?"

"OK, Sarge."

The two men sat down on a couple of wooden ammunition boxes that served as chairs and set their weapons and helmets to one side. "Sorry I slept so long, Sergeant. It must have been four hours."

"That's OK, sir. You looked so peaceful that I didn't have the heart to wake you," the sergeant replied with a smile.

The lieutenant spoke in a serious tone, "How are the men doing, in your opinion?"

"They are fine right now; we had three KIA and about eight wounded."

"I didn't know we lost three."

"The two ROKs in DiAngelo's squad didn't make it, and with Anderson, that makes three."

"You say seven WIA?"

"Yeah, two should be coming back. They were pretty minor hits. The boys tell me that you were a fighting fool, Lieutenant; they said you nailed at least eight chinks."

"You know, Sergeant, things were happening so fast I really didn't think about what I was doing. I probably should have been directing the fire of the men."

"Well, I don't know about that, Lieutenant. DiAngelo says he has never seen anyone handle a rifle like you did."

"I appreciate your confidence," the platoon leader quietly said.

"The men were really impressed, Lieutenant. I think you set them quite an example."

The lieutenant spoke again in a serious manner. "What do you think of our situation, Sergeant?"

"Do you want my honest opinion, Sir?"

"Yes, I do."

"I think we are in one hell of a tight spot. I heard from one of the guys at Battalion that the 3rd Battalion of the 31st was just about overrun last night, and they are with two batteries of the 57th Field Artillery and several tracks from the 15th AAA. He also told me that according to what he heard from S-2, the chinks have four whole divisions on this side of the reservoir and that they are going to try to wipe us out. He said that a Chinese prisoner told them that there were four more divisions that are going to try to knock out the entire 1st Marine Division. Frankly, Sir, I'm scared to death. You know, I was in the Pacific in the infantry, and I saw some fighting, but I never saw anything like this. The chink infantry just keeps coming. It looks to me like they just keep throwing in more men until they finally just walk over you."

There was a minute of silence. The two men stared at the bare earth of the bunker floor. "I appreciate your candor, Sergeant Pratt. Another thing, I think you're doing a terrific job. It's obvious to me that your leadership really paid off last night. We're lucky to have you on board!"

"Thank you, sir. I hope you feel the same way after we get out of this rat trap."

"What should we do now while it's still light, Sergeant?" asked the lieutenant.

"Well, we're in pretty good shape in terms of ammunition. I would suggest that you personally talk to each man. I think it would mean a lot to the men. They think you're something of a hero. Other than that, the platoon is ready to go. We passed out at least three grenades to each man. I checked for frostbite. It doesn't look like it's a problem. Cobb has been working on those guns all morning, and he has enough ammo to fight off the whole chink army. You might see what you think of making a minor change in the location of the guns. It might be something that would surprise the chinks. The morale is pretty high. I have been telling everybody that we will hold until the rest of the 31st Infantry gets here. I've been keeping my worries to myself."

46

The platoon sergeant and the lieutenant sat for a few minutes in silence. "I think we are going to get hit again tonight, sir, and I hope we can hold them off." More silence. The dim light in the bunker outlined the serious faces of the two men. "There is something else you might like to know, Lieutenant. This morning General Almond, the X Corps commander, landed here by chopper. He conferred with Colonel Faith and Colonel MacLean, and after that, he pinned the Silver Star on Colonel Faith. As soon as the general left, Colonel Faith tore off the medal and threw it in the snow," the platoon sergeant related.

"Why do you suppose he did that, Sergeant?" the lieutenant asked.

"I don't know, but Colonel Faith must be really unhappy about something. It's not like him to do something like that." Silence.

"I'm glad General Almond didn't find me sleeping, Sergeant."

"We would have woken you before he got here. I told Polowski to be on the alert for any brass," the platoon sergeant answered with a grin.

The runner, Private First-Class Elmer C. Polowski, crawled through the bunker doorway. "Come on in, Polowski," the platoon sergeant called.

"The cooks are making some stew and coffee for supper," the runner reported

"That sounds good to me, men," the platoon leader responded enthusiastically. "Sergeant Pratt, would you take charge of getting the platoon fed?"

"Yes, Sir, I'll get right on it," the platoon sergeant replied.

"I'll start walking the line," the lieutenant stated.

The platoon leader started slowly moving along the line of irregular trenches and foxholes. The enemy activity had dropped off significantly, but some portions of the perimeter were still receiving sporadic long-range rifle fire. The lieutenant went to each man. "How is it going, Soldier? Is your weapon working OK? We are going to get some hot food for supper."

The men, for the most part, seemed confident and assured, but there was a kind of uncertainty that ran through the platoon. They had questions: "Are the Marines going to relieve us, Sir?" Will we be moving tomorrow?"

"We are holding until further orders," the lieutenant stated.

More men commented. "The hot chow sounds good to me." "You sure gave them hell last night."

John Schneidermann replied with a slight smile, "Not quite that many."

At the machine gun position, all was particularly tidy. "Sergeant Cobb, I think we should shift the guns to the left. The goal is to confuse the enemy. If they have our crew-served weapons plotted, they might concentrate on them. Moving the guns will avoid that possibility."

"Yes, Suh, ah, understand your idea on that. Ah was kinda' thinkin' about the same thing myself. Ah was thinkin' of right over there, Suh," said the squad leader.

"Looks good, Sergeant. Make your move just before dark."

"Yes, Suh."

It took quite some time to contact each man on the line, but the platoon leader stuck to his task. The men seemed to welcome the attention and tried to make the visit last. *Don't go, Dad; tell me a story, Dad; leave the light on, Dad,* he thought.

The platoon slipped away to the kitchen, a few men at a time. The last rays of light began to fade over the battalion perimeter. The temperature was dropping as the light dimmed. At the platoon Command Post, the five members of the headquarters group met. The runner, the medic, and the assistant platoon sergeant had eaten first, and after their return, Sergeant Pratt and the lieutenant walked to the kitchen tent. The company kitchen crew was working under a canvas fly and a squad tent. They had, through extreme effort, cooked a delicious stew. The aroma from the main dish floated over the immediate area. The stew consisted of pieces of beef, vegetables, noodles, and an aggregation of other ingredients. The hot stew and the steaming coffee were well-received by the men of the company. As the daylight finally faded, the kitchen closed down for the night.

At the platoon CP, the headquarters group assembled inside the bunker. The burning candle created dancing shadows on the crude interior of the structure. As the men sipped coffee from their canteen cups, the platoon leader opened the meeting: "It's very possible that the enemy could hit us again tonight. Our orders are to hold our position. In the event of an attack, Sergeant Pratt will take a position on the left by the machine gun. I will take a position with the 2nd squad. Thanks to the platoon sergeant, we now have two more phones. He and I will each take one with us to our positions on the line. The runner laid the wire up there this afternoon. We will have a direct line to the 81s and possibly the 4.2s. If it looks like an attack, we will call in as much mortar fire as possible. Rideout, Polowski, and Garza will stay here at the CP and be prepared to move on order.

In case the phones go dead, you three report to me. It looks like we are facing a large Chinese force. It will probably take some time for the division to regroup and stabilize the situation. It is a fact that we are surrounded, but with everyone doing his job, we are going to come through in good order. Any further comments, Sergeant Pratt?"

The sergeant cleared his throat and began speaking, "I told all the men that it's important to make every shot count. Wait till you see a target. Don't get rattled and shoot wildly. The squad leaders have all been told this already. There's no rag-tag enemy that can stand up to the firepower of the U.S. Infantry if everyone keeps cool. Machine guns and automatic rifles should only fire on massed targets. Leave the probers to the rifles."

A whistle came over the phone. "3rd Platoon," answered the runner. "It's for you, Sir. The CO."

The lieutenant spoke into the receiver, "Schneidermann, Sir."

The company commander spoke in measured tones, "I'm checking all the platoons. Is everything all set?"

The lieutenant replied, "Yes, Sir. We are all in position, the ammunition supply is OK, and the men are in good spirits."

The company commander continued in a serious voice, "It sounds like the 3rd Battalion of the 31st really got clobbered, and they are under attack now. They have some quad .50s and some twin 40s, too. OK, Lieutenant, stay on the ball and keep in touch."

"Yes, Sir."

The platoon sergeant continued speaking, "Another thing we better get straight--these chink soldiers are no amateurs. They are tough, and they are disciplined. There is an old saying in the infantry: You can't beat Davy Crockett with a Boy Scout.

Well, these chinks are no Boy Scouts. I have four extra rifles. I test-fired them today, and they work fine. If you see anyone who needs a good rifle, gets one of these over to him. I'll leave them in the CP. Any other comments?" the platoon leader asked. No one spoke. The lieutenant spoke again, "Why don't some of you men get some sleep? I'm going up to the line."

All was quiet on the firing line. The squad position included four men: the squad leader, two riflemen, and an automatic rifleman. Two men, the squad leader, and a rifleman, were awake--

actually wide awake. The platoon leader slid into the trench beside the sergeant. "Everything OK, Sergeant?"

"It's been pretty quiet so far. We're trying to keep a sharp watch. We just haven't seen any movement."

"I'm going to get the phone working." The lieutenant clipped the phone ends to the two wires that were tied to a stake. He gave a low whistle.

The runner, Polowski, answered, "Third platoon."

"Checking the line. This is the lieutenant."

The position fell silent again as the men in the emplacement stared intently into the darkness. An hour slipped by without any activity in front of the line. The only sound above the wind was the occasional distant artillery fire and the labored breathing of the sleeping soldiers.

Thoughts crowd into the mind during the silence of the night. The images of the last few days blazed into view--the enemy attacking from the shadows, the arctic blasts of cold, the snow, the wounded trying to hobble to the rear, and the flash of weapons firing in the darkness. It all seemed unreal, but it was only too real.

Second Lieutenant John W. Schneidermann reached into his jacket and felt the .45 automatic that was in a shoulder holster on his left side just over his left shirt pocket. It was loaded with a round in the chamber and a full magazine. Three, extra, loaded magazines were tucked into his jacket pockets.

# Leaving

Between father and son, a bond existed that was never obvious but was always present. The summer had been difficult with the excessive rain. The tractors had more than a little trouble getting through the soft fields. After the planting was done, the growing season took a turn for the better. While moisture was still a problem, the crops had grown miraculously. Now, as the fall approached, the prospects of a reasonably good harvest were there.

"Well, John, I suppose we will have to get you to the train tomorrow."

"I'm afraid so, Dad."

"I sure hate to see you go, Son."

"I would just as soon stay, but the Army might not see it that way."

"By the way, John, you could take the old .45 if you want to. I carried it in France in the Rainbow Division."

"That would be great, Dad, if you think you want to let it go."

"Yeah, you better take it. Just look at it as an insurance policy."

The train was standing beside the red-brick paved station platform. The coaches looked drab. The passenger trains of the day appeared dingy with their dirty windows and with steam rising from under the cars. Only a handful of people were waiting to board.

"You change at Omaha. Is that right?"

"That's right, Dad."

Passengers were climbing the steps to the coaches. The young officer in a well-pressed, suntan, summer uniform picked up his light traveling bag.

"Have a good trip, Son."

"You take care, Dad. Hope the weather straightens out." He gave a half-wave, half-salute, and bounded up the steps into the coach and was out of sight.

# Night

The darkness became more intense, hiding all the familiar features that were so clearly visible during the day. The men on the line felt their sense of night vision improve. An increasing wind, together with light snow, made observing more difficult. The squad leader turned and softly whispered, "Do you see anything?"

"Not a thing, Sergeant. Maybe we'll get lucky." The platoon leader opened the brown leather case and took out a pair of standard, infantry 6x30 binoculars. Observing with field glasses gave a more distinct view of the night terrain. The lieutenant thought: *It might be that the Chinese have had enough. It could be that they are heading back up north, though not likely if they are attacking the 31st right now. I wonder if there is something that should be checked. You can check things only so many times. I better get back to the CP and report in to the company.*

The platoon leader walked back toward the CP, carefully picking his way through the darkness. Inside, the assistant platoon sergeant was sitting by the phone. The lieutenant picked up the receiver and gave a low whistle.

"CP," the first sergeant answered.

"Schneidermann reporting in. Everything's quiet. I've just been on the line, and nothing is moving that we can see."

"OK, Lieutenant. All the other platoons are reporting the same."

The platoon leader sat down on a wooden ammunition box and leaned back against the dirt wall of the bunker. "What's happening at the CP, Sergeant?"

"Pretty quiet, sir. I've been reporting in about every half hour, and I've been keeping the mortars on the line, too."

"Sounds good."

The other two men were lying against the wall of the bunker, curled up in their sleeping bags, looking like oversized cocoons. Their measured breathing was audible in the silence of the emplacement.

"Where are you from, Sergeant Ridehout?" the lieutenant inquired.

"I'm from Pennsylvania, Sir."

"How is everything going with you?" the lieutenant continued.

"About as well as can be expected, Sir. I've the Army. I hope things will work out so I can stay in. This kind of combat is tough, but we should see it through. I came from sort of a bad home situation, Sir. I was glad to leave. The Army has always treated me OK, Sir. I hope that I'm doing the job for you," Ridehout answered, his words flowing like water from a broken dam. The normally quiet sergeant poured out his past in a continuous stream. The story was not always pretty. It touched on alcoholism, abuse, and other sordid facets of human nature.

At last, the young soldier stopped talking and stared blankly at the floor. The platoon leader had listened intently to the sergeant's story, not commenting or interrupting. "Sorry to bore you with my problems, Sir," the sergeant said.

"Not at all, Sergeant. I was happy to listen, and I must say that I am well satisfied with your performance. Sergeant Pratt has mentioned on several occasions that he feels that you're doing a good job. I value the platoon sergeant's opinion very highly," the lieutenant stated emphatically.

Sergeant Ridehout looked up with a relieved expression. "Thank you, Sir. I won't let you down."

The young officer reached over and gave the non-com a light slap on the shoulder. "You're doing fine." After a brief silence, the lieutenant spoke, "I'm going to try and get a little sleep. Wake me up if anything happens."

"Yes, Sir."

In a short time, the platoon leader dropped into an uneasy sleep. This time he kept all his clothes and boots on. The men of the platoon maintained a tense vigil with all hands on alert. As the night wore on and it appeared that no action would take place, a portion of the men tried to get some much-needed sleep. Toward midnight the situation dramatically changed.

# Shadows

At the machine gun squad, the platoon sergeant was in position and on watch. A distinct feeling of dread was gnawing at his psyche. Something was amiss, and he just couldn't put a handle on it. Without any particular reason, he called the CP. "Let me talk to the Lieutenant."

Sergeant Ridehout leaned over and lightly shook the platoon leader, "Phone, Sir." The platoon leader lurched to a sitting position, rubbed his face, and reached for the phone.

The platoon sergeant's voice came over the wire, sounding strange and far away, "This is Pratt. I can't explain it, but something doesn't look right. Maybe you could come up here."

The platoon leader scrambled out of his sleeping bag, "I'll be right there." He picked up his rifle and headed out of the doorway of the bunker. Within a few short minutes, he made it to the machine gun squad position, where the machine guns were strongly situated in bunkers originally constructed by the 5th Marines. There were three main occupied positions: two held three men and a light .30 caliber gun, and the other was manned by the squad leader and the platoon sergeant.

"Sorry to shake you out, Lieutenant."

"That's OK. What do you think is out there?"

"I just can't put my finger on it, but I've got a bad feeling."

The platoon leader scanned the front with his binoculars. "I don't see a thing, but maybe we should call for a flare." With a low whistle, the lieutenant raised the company CP. "Put me through to the 81st," he ordered.

"We think there's enemy to our front. Could you fire Concentrations 5 and 6?"

"On the way," came the report from the 81mm Mortar Platoon. In less than a minute, the mortars fired a three-round volley. The flight of the rounds formed an arc overhead and came crashing down in front of the rifle platoon. Over the sound of the wind came excited cries that could be heard at the machine gun position.

"They're out there, all right!" shouted the platoon sergeant.

"I think you're right. I heard them, too!" the lieutenant exclaimed.

Several minutes of silence followed as the men in the gun position listened carefully. The platoon leader called again to the mortar platoon, "I think we hit some enemy with that barrage."

"Good show! Shall we fire again?" was the reply.

"Let's hold fire for now. Can you stay on the line?"

"We'll stay on for now."

All was silent at the platoon front.

The platoon leader spoke in a low voice, "I better move over to the 2nd Squad and see what it looks like from there." The lieutenant slowly and carefully walked to the second squad position. "How is it going, Sergeant?"

"Fine, Lieutenant. What were the blasts out in front of us?"

"We had the mortars fire a concentration. We think they hit something."

The squad leader slowly nodded his head. "What do you think is going to happen, Lieutenant?"

"I wish I knew. There's a good chance that they will hit us again, but we're in better shape tonight." Both men continued to peer intently into the darkness, straining to pick up any hint of movement. After more minutes of silence, only the wind gave a slight stirring noise.

Sergeant DiAngelo was the first to notice the moving shadow. He punched the platoon leader and pointed. The enemy had started their attack with individual skirmishers probing for weak spots in the infantry line. Several rifles cracked almost at once. The riflemen of the platoon began mounting a steady, deliberate fire. No automatic weapons started firing. The entire battalion perimeter now came to life as the noise of battle rose to a high pitch. The enemy skirmishers dropped back, and firing slowed. After a lull of several minutes, the Chinese infantry launched a massive assault at numerous places on the battalion line. On the platoon front, the situation was tense. The men were on their feet, in position, and firing rapidly. The massive firepower was having a disastrous effect on the attacking infantry. The noise of the conflict rose to a high pitch as the supporting weapons joined in the fight. At the second squad position, the men swung into action. The automatic rifle team was working well. The AR man was methodically sweeping the squad front, firing three-and four-round bursts at the moving shadows. The rifleman serving as the AR's backup was by his side, calmly passing full magazines as they were needed. The basic load for a Browning Automatic Rifle was 400 rounds loaded in 20-round magazines which were normally carried by two men. The platoon leader was closely observing but not firing. The other rifleman in the squad position was crouching in one corner of the trench. Although his rifle was lying across the parapet, he did not appear to be firing.

Second Lieutenant John W. Schneidermann moved to a point immediately behind the soldier. After watching for a few seconds, he crawled into the position right beside the rifleman. "Why aren't you firing, Soldier?" the lieutenant asked in a sharp voice.

The man looked around, surprised at seeing the officer. A blank look came over his already pale face. "I don't know," he murmured.

"Get that rifle up to your shoulder and start shooting," the lieutenant barked.

With some hesitation, the man complied. The rifle cracked once and then again.

"Keep that up, Soldier. You're doing fine." The platoon leader stayed by the rifleman, who was now methodically firing at a slow, steady rate. "Don't let up, Soldier. You can do it. Remember the firing range."

The battalion was now hard-pressed by the massive enemy assaults. They would launch an attack with odds more than four to one. When a charge was broken up by the deadly hail of high-velocity fire, the tenacious soldiers of the People's Liberation Army would reform and launch yet another determined assault. The ever-present cold, the flashes of fire, the incessant chatter of small arms, and the piercing bugle notes created a scene from the inferno.

The telephone line to the company CP went dead, a casualty of the incoming mortar fire. Shortly after, the runner and the assistant platoon sergeant presented themselves to the platoon leader at his position on the firing line.

The platoon leader turned to Sergeant Ridehout, "Go back to the 81st mortar platoon and request that they fire all the concentrations to our front. Have them fire as much as possible. After you have done that, contact the 60s and the 4.2s, and have them give us all the fire they can spare on the same targets. Polowski, see if you can get that phone working."

Both men slipped away, keeping as low as possible.

The platoon had now repulsed several attacks that had occurred about every thirty to forty minutes. The assaults had continued with unrelenting ferocity. The enemy would attack, be forced back, regroup, reinforce, then attack again. The strain of such sustained action was beginning to tell on the infantry soldiers of the rifle platoon.

It was 1862, and Fredericksburg all over again--waves of massed infantry attacking entrenched defenders. This time the defenders were vastly outnumbered. The attackers, in their quilted uniforms and with their bugle calls, continued attacking relentlessly. After each effort by the Chinese, the battalion shook and shuddered like a ship buffeted by a storm.

The battalion commander, Lieutenant Colonel Don Carlos Faith, USA, was tense as he sat in the mud and thatched house that served as the command post. The CO of the 31st Infantry, Colonel Allan D. MacLean, who was the commander of the RCT, was also present. The staff officers and the two commanders were listening to the reports from the companies as they came in. The officers were worried. In recent battles in the Eighth Army sector, the 3rd Battalion of the 8th U.S. Cavalry had been virtually annihilated by the forces of the PLA. This event was weighing heavily on their minds. This fight was rapidly taking on the appearance of that disaster, and the entire headquarters knew it.

The platoon was holding, but pressure was building. About fifteen minutes after the departure of the assistant platoon sergeant, mortar rounds began falling in front of the platoon line. The ground shook as a concert of exploding shells crashed in a series of blasts. This broke up an enemy attack that was in the process of forming. This, in turn, relieved the riflemen on the line.

While John Schneidermann's platoon was doing reasonably well, things were not good with the battalion. After about two hours of intense combat, the fighting ability of the unit was weakening. The Battalion Commander, with the concurrence of the Commander of the 31st RCT, decided to break out of the position. The goal would be to link up with the other battalion, the 3rd of the 31st Infantry, which was defending a perimeter of its own less than four miles down the road to the south.

The platoon leader was in a high state of exhilaration. The defense of the platoon line had gone well. The platoon was fighting like a team and winning. Each enemy infantry assault had been beaten back with heavy losses on the enemy side. The mortar barrage had caught them at a critical time, which had seriously shaken the resolve of the Chinese rifle company. The platoon leader did a better job than the night before. He kept in contact with each squad with dash and enthusiasm. The men had taken heart from the outstanding display of leadership.

The runner, PFC Polowski, appeared through the darkness at the squad position and reported, "I haven't been able to find the break in the wire yet, Sir. I stopped at the company CP, and they say we are going to move out tonight."

"Are you sure about that?" the lieutenant asked.

"Yes, Sir. I was there when the call came through, and the CO answered it. He said the battalion is going to fight its way south to where the 31st is at."

"We better keep trying to get that phone working. Maybe we better see about laying a new line. If we don't have enough wire on the spool, get some from the commo people."

"Yes, Sir, I'll take right off."

Action on the platoon line began picking up. Bugles were sounding, and the enemy mortars began falling within the platoon sector. Again, the shadows were moving to the front of the soldiers of the 7th Infantry Division. Through the confusion, the platoon sergeant suddenly popped up at the 2nd Squad position.

"Good to see you, Sergeant. How's it going at the machine guns?" asked the platoon leader.

"Still holding, but, man, this is the wildest thing I've ever seen! There's just no end to the chinks. The guns have been working well. Cobb's on top of things, but, man, this is unbelievable!" The platoon sergeant was definitely shaken.

The platoon leader spoke. "Polowski says that he heard that the battalion is going to pull out and move south to link up with the 3rd Battalion of the 31st. We better get ready if the word does come down to move. Sergeant Pratt, you move back to the CP bunker. Polowski's trying to get the phone going, but, if necessary, you report to the company and find out what's going on."

"OK, Lieutenant."

The lieutenant put his arm over the shoulder of the older man and spoke in a quiet voice, "Now you move out and get hold of the situation. We all need your help."

The platoon sergeant looked directly at the young officer with a perplexed expression. "Yes, Sir. I'll get going right now."

The young infantry lieutenant had become something of a solid rock. After an initial night of confusion and indecision, he reverted to a tower of determined action. He had been in constant contact with his squads with encouragement and solid direction. He gave orders, and the men responded. The situation was desperate, and the conditions adverse, but the young officer was in command. The platoon was fighting like a wild animal locked in a life-and-death struggle in the primeval wilderness. The blood of his ancestors had again risen to the surface, those unknown warriors who had fought for survival in a world where conflict and destruction were commonplace and where only the fittest survived.

A silent figure approached from the rear. Sergeant Ridehout, the assistant platoon sergeant, slipped into the squad position. He asked in a loud whisper, "Sir, did the mortar fire do any good?"

"Right on target, Sergeant. You did a great job."

The sergeant continued, "I was at the 81st, and they are going to keep firing the concentrations on a regular schedule. I talked to the 4.2s by phone, and they said they would do their best but couldn't promise anything. The 60s were going to fire, too. Are we going to move out of here, Sir?"

"I don't know for sure, but Sergeant Pratt is checking it out now."

As the two men talked, the rifle squad was keeping up a deliberate fire, steady but not frantic. "Sergeant Ridehout, check with the squads and see what their ammunition supply is. There is some rifle ammo at the CP bunker. Take some bandoliers with you and give them out."

"Yes, Sir. I'll get rolling right away."

As the sergeant left, heading toward the CP, the lieutenant thought: *The situation is getting critical. There just doesn't seem to be any let up. Are these guys ever going to quit attacking! I hope the boys can hold out.*

The end rifleman was still firing methodically, resolutely. The platoon leader crawled over to the fighter. "How's it going, Soldier?"

The rifleman grinned, "I'm giving them hell, just like you told me to."

Ready on the right, ready on the left, flag is up, flag is waving, flag is down, targets up. Commence firing! The familiar language of the rifle range comes to mind from the past. Sergeant DiAngelo moved to the platoon leader's side, "What's going to happen, Lieutenant?"

The platoon leader replied, "We're going to hang in there, Sergeant. We're beating them. Just keep up the fire. Your squad is looking first rate."

The assistant platoon sergeant approached from the left of the line, ducking low, hugging the ground.

"How are things on the left, Sergeant?"

"The line is holding, but the Chinks just keep coming. The ammo is getting low down there. I am going to take some more out to the line."

"OK, could you use some more help?"

"Yeah, that would be good," the sergeant answered.

The lieutenant moved to the squad leader. "Sergeant DiAngelo, send a man back with Ridehout to pick up some more bandoliers." The squad leader crawled to the end rifleman and directed him back toward the assistant platoon sergeant. The two men glided off into the blackness of the cold night.

The platoon leader paused to catch his breath. He thought: *The battle has been going on for nearly four hours with the enemy mounting attacks at regular intervals. This whole thing is a nightmare: the darkness, the blowing snow, the bugles, the noise.*

The beleaguered soldiers of the 7th Division knew that they were in a deadly contest and that there was no place to run. It was fight or die, and so the platoon hunkered down and kept up a steady fire as the shadow figures came on again and still again. The firepower of the platoon was awesome, with six automatic rifles, two light machine guns, and twenty some rifles. They were capable of putting out an excess of 2000 aimed shots per minute.

No massed infantry could stand against such a hail of high velocity .30 caliber bullets. The platoon would lose its punch, however, when worn down by casualties, fatigue, cold, and lack of ammunition. The picture emerges of a powerful buffalo bull surrounded by a pack of wolves, relentlessly attacking, trying to wear down the magnificent monarch of the prairies.

# Pull Out

The runner, Polowski, emerged from the curtain of blowing snow and spoke to the lieutenant in a breathless whisper, "Sir, we laid a new line, and the phone is working. The CO wants to talk to you."

The platoon leader picked up the sound-powered phone, "Hello, Schneidermann, we are going to pull out and join the 31st. The company will act as the rear guard. We'll start moving in about a half hour. Keep the phone manned, and we will keep you informed." The company commander continued, "How are your boys holding?"

"We are hanging on OK. I think we can keep our position for a while."

"Good. How many casualties have you taken?"

"I'm not exactly sure, sir, but I think four KIA and seven WIA."

"OK, keep on holding."

The prospect of movement stirred the men of the command group into action. The platoon leader slipped back to the CP bunker, closely followed by the runner. The assistant platoon sergeant and the rifleman came along a few minutes later. Inside the bunker, the platoon sergeant was sitting in one corner with the phone in his hand. The five men formed a tight circle around the flickering candle.

The platoon leader began speaking, "The CO has given the order that we are going to pull out in about thirty minutes. The company will act as the rear guard for the battalion. We'll move south down the road to where the 31st is holding. When we get the signal to move, the two flank squads will pull out first, then the machine guns and the 2nd Squad. The platoon sergeant will move out with the first two squads, and the rest of us will move with the second two. We will lay down a heavy volume of fire just before leaving the positions." The lieutenant continued, "Right now, I want all of you to take the rest of the ammunition and move up to the line. Sergeant Ridehout, check the left flank squad. Sergeant Pratt, check the machine guns. Polowski and I will check the two right flank squads. Make sure that you give the squad leaders the order about pulling out. Are there any questions? If not, let's get moving."

The men in the bunker moved with renewed vigor. After dividing up the remaining bandoliers and looping them over their shoulders, they headed for the firing line. "Polowski, you stay here on the phone until I get to the squad position," the lieutenant ordered.

"Yes, Sir."

Singly the men moved toward the line, hampered by the darkness and the rough terrain. When he reached the squad position, the platoon leader conferred with Sergeant DiAngelo, giving him the details of the planned withdrawal. The squad leader's face formed a twisted smile, "You know, I don't feel too bad about leaving."

"I would agree, Sergeant," the platoon leader replied. After a brief check of the squad position, the lieutenant worked his way to the right flank squad. There he repeated the orders for the withdrawal and dropped off the last of the bandoliers. "Do you have any questions, O'Malley?" he asked.

"It sounds clear to me. When we get the word to pull out, we lay down a base of fire and then move out to the road and report to Sergeant Pratt," the squad leader replied.

"That's right. How has your squad held up so far?" the lieutenant asked.

"Well, not too bad. I have two guys hurt, but not too serious. I think they will be able to keep going. That mortar fire really helped. I think that last barrage did a lot of damage. It seemed to slow up that last attack."

Second Lieutenant John W. Schneidermann slipped back to the 2nd Squad position, picked up the phone, and gave a low whistle.

"Third Platoon. This is Polowski."

"Bring up the ammo," the platoon leader ordered.

"OK, Lieutenant."

A whistle came over the phone. "This is the 3rd Platoon," the lieutenant answered.

A voice sounding strained and distant came through the handset. "Are you ready to move out?" the voice asked.

"We are ready when we get the word," the platoon leader responded.

One of the most difficult movements that any military unit may be called upon to execute is a withdrawal in the face of an enemy attack. For the platoon as well as the entire battalion, the maneuver was complicated by the adverse weather conditions, poor communications, a lack of training in withdrawal techniques, and the overwhelming numerical superiority of a determined enemy. The most critical time during a withdrawal, the time when the risk is greatest, is when the unit is in the act of physically leaving its defensive positions. At that time, if the enemy makes an all-out attack, the enemy's chances of success are favorable. Surprisingly, it was as the platoon was making ready to abandon their entrenchments that the enemy attacks began to slacken. As in most situations, the success or failure of men or nations can ride on a turn of fate. On the night of November 28th and 29th, the god of battle indeed smiled on the platoon.

Sometime after 0500, the message came over the phone, "Move out. Move out." The platoon acknowledged the order and immediately sent word to the left flank squad via the platoon runner. The lieutenant moved carefully to the right flank squad and gave the order to begin pulling back. An increased volume of fire on each flank signaled that the movement was in motion. The riflemen began shuffling toward the roadway as the squads started moving.

The men resembled bears with their load of equipment and their winter gear. The sky was still pitch black in the pre-dawn hours. The platoon sergeant emerged from the darkness. "I'll head out to the road, Lieutenant," the sergeant called out.

"Good show, Sergeant. We'll be right behind you."

"I heard that the First Platoon is cut off and can't get out," Sergeant Pratt continued.

The young officer felt a sinking feeling in the pit of his stomach as he turned to the assistant platoon sergeant. "Get over to the machine guns and tell Sergeant Cobb to start pulling out," he continued.

"Right away, Sir," the sergeant acknowledged as he moved off into the darkness. Within a few minutes came the sound of the rapid firing of the light .30s. "OK, DiAngelo, let's get going," ordered the platoon leader. The automatic rifles of the squad cut loose with several short bursts.

Second Lieutenant John W. Schneidermann started down the short trail to the road. The runner followed closely like a hunting hound. "Be sure and take the phones, Polowski," the lieutenant called.

"I have them, Sir, and a wire spool," the runner replied.

In the darkness, the confusion of battle compounds. The platoon moved in starts and stops, a ragged column slipping and sliding as they headed south. The men were apprehensive but not panicky. They had taken their equipment and ammunition. Little was left to an always hungry and ill-equipped enemy. Left in the positions they had been defending were the members of the platoon that had been killed during the night. They were relieved of their ammunition, and their weapons were disabled. A quick salute was their final tribute there in a hostile land far from family and home.

Once on the road, the platoon leader stopped to observe as the last of the platoon ambled by. Last of all came the machine gun squad, a gun crew on each side of the road. The squad leader of the machine guns was with the crews on the road, giving orders, moving back and forth, and making sure everyone was accounted for. "Good mawnin', Suh," was his cheerful greeting.

"Good morning to you, Sergeant. How's it going?" the platoon leader inquired.

"Just fine, Suh. Both guns are working good, and we have four boxes for each gun," the squad leader replied.

"Very good, Sergeant."

The platoon now passed through the battalion CP area, which was littered with the debris of battle--disabled vehicles, weapons, cardboard boxes, and all forms of discarded supplies and material. The men of the platoon kept moving. A certain optimism accompanies movement. The vision of better times gives the fighting soldier hope and, with hope, renewal, and inner strength to accomplish whatever it takes to keep going.

The road ran straight south down the valley toward the reservoir, and the turned sharply northeast along the north side of an inlet channel. The inlet stream, known as the Pungnyuri-gang, flowed into the lake from the east. As the men continued their southward movement, light from the new dawn slowly streaked over the eastern hills. As the light strengthened, the terrain features became more distinct, and the figures of the walking infantrymen emerged from the shadows.

The Chinese had not followed the departing battalion. For some unknown reason, they had held back, not moving as the daylight continued to brighten the battlefield. After some time, the dark figures of the enemy riflemen could be seen in the distance. The machine gunners stopped periodically and fired at the visible Chinese soldiers. The supporting heavy mortars also provided an effective covering These powerful weapons, with a shell equal in explosive force to a 105mm howitzer round, started dropping charges among the pursuing enemy with telling effect.

The movement south by the 1st Battalion went reasonably well. The sixty-odd trucks of the battalion, many containing wounded, were able to travel the relatively short distance without being hindered by the enemy. The two rifle companies in the lead were able to march forward comparatively free from enemy attack. The column moved at a snail's pace, but by 0900, the point units were in position to cross a causeway and a bridge into the perimeter of the 3rd Battalion, 31st Infantry, and their supporting artillery batteries.

The platoon, now on the road, was moving as a team. The men were strung out on both sides of the dirt road for about a hundred yards with the remainder of the company directly ahead. Second Lieutenant John Schneidermann was in the middle of the roadway in close contact with the two rear squads.

The dusty track was perched on the toe of a large hill mass that ran north and south, the peaks of which reached over 260 meters above the level of the reservoir. The road was fairly level but quite crooked. The main body of the battalion could be seen ahead at the point where the road turned east. The scenery was majestic, with rugged hills, the wide-open spaces of the frozen reservoir, and the frozen streams. The men of the platoon were not thinking of scenery but of the safety of the defensive perimeter beyond the inlet. As the rear guard rapidly closed on the main body, the enemy forces were, in turn, narrowing their distance to the rear guard.

At such a critical time, when the battalion was threatened by a mass infantry attack, out of the sky roared a flight of supporting Marine aircraft. The Corsairs, one at a time, came streaking in to strike the pursuing Chinese forces. The men of the platoon cheered as the aircraft hit the enemy with a fiery burst of napalm. The platoon, along with the rest of the company, was now in contact with the main body of the battalion. As they waited for the lead elements of the battalion to break through to the defensive perimeter, they formed a skirmish line across the road as a precaution against a renewed enemy attack. The two machine guns were set up and loaded, one on each side of the road. They were in a position to sweep the approaches to the platoon position.

The men sat down and tried to relax as they gnawed at cold C-Rations. The platoon leader called his two senior non-coms together for an impromptu conference right on the side of the road. "How did the movement go, men?" he asked in a voice colored with fatigue.

The platoon sergeant spoke up, "It went better than I thought it possibly could go; the first two squads moved like clockwork."

"I agree with that," the lieutenant replied. "Were there any casualties?"

The sergeant answered, "Two of the ROKs disappeared; nobody knows what happened. They must have gotten lost in the dark, or they just didn't get the word. I sure will be glad to see some artillery support. Maybe with some more firepower, we can keep the chinks off our backs."

The platoon leader continued, "How is the frostbite situation?"

The platoon sergeant answered, "It looks OK."

The lieutenant spoke in a subdued voice, "You two stay here and make a quick check on the men while I report to the company." The platoon leader hiked up the road to where the company commander was standing by a command jeep. Four other men from the company headquarters were nearby.

"Just the man I wanted to see. How are you doing back there, Schneidermann?" the CO asked in a cheery voice.

"We're doing fine, Sir," the lieutenant answered.

"You and your people are doing great. Keep up the good work," the CO urged.

"What is the plan, Sir?" the lieutenant asked.

"I haven't heard much, Lieutenant. I am assuming that we are all going into the perimeter and setting up a defensive position. With all the firepower they have there, we should be able to hold out in good order."

Second Lieutenant John W. Schneidermann walked back to the northernmost part of the column, where the platoon was stretched across the road. The men were sprawled in a wide variety of relaxed poses. The vacant, numbed facial expressions reflected the intensity of the recent combat.

After some time, the column began to move at a slow walk. The platoon maintained its position and the same formation. The ragged train of men and vehicles moved forward a short distance, stopped, and then started and stopped again. Finally, the platoon rounded the big bend in the road and could see the defensive positions of the other infantry battalion.

66

The platoon kept moving, starting, stopping, getting ever closer to the new position. The men could hear firing from across the frozen arm of the reservoir that separated them from the 31st Infantry perimeter. From the bend in the road to the bridge crossing, the inlet was a distance of about one mile. This stretch of narrow dirt track was bounded on the north by a steep hill mass and on the south by the inlet to the reservoir, which was about a quarter mile wide. The men of the platoon moved along deliberately in a manner characteristic of veteran infantry: keeping spread out, observing the terrain, with weapons at the ready. The enemy had given up its pursuit of the column and, except for a few brief encounters, had not been visible. As the platoon moved closer to the perimeter, it became increasingly apparent that the position was under attack. Instead of a refuge, it looked like the area was the scene of a desperate battle.

As the platoon made a stop, Sergeant Pratt came running back to where the lieutenant was kneeling in the south road ditch, observing with his binoculars. The platoon sergeant was breathing hard as he flopped into the ditch alongside the young officer. "How does this thing look to you, Lieutenant?"

"It doesn't look good. I can see the chinks coming down from the hills to the south; it looks like there is some fire coming from the valley to the east of the bridge," the lieutenant said as he handed the glasses to the platoon sergeant.

"This looks like a hell of a mess to me, Lieutenant," the sergeant exclaimed. The platoon sergeant shouted excitedly, "Look at those quad .50s shoot! I sure don't like the looks of this, Lieutenant. I thought we were getting into a strong position. It looks worse than what we left. Did you hear about Colonel MacLean?"

"No, I didn't," replied the platoon leader.

"He disappeared right south of where we are right now. He tried to cross on the ice by himself and was captured."

"Are you sure?" the lieutenant asked with a puzzled expression.

"I got it right from the Sergeant Major," the platoon sergeant asserted. Second Lieutenant John W. Schneidermann took a deep breath and stared off in the direction of the battle scene. It was an unbelievable picture: massed formations of stocky, hardy soldiers in padded uniforms pouring down the bleak slopes of the hills to the south, a cluttered array of

Americans fighting for their lives, the tracked gun carriages spitting a rapid volume of machine gun and cannon fire, smoke covering the action like a filmy cloak. It was like being a spectator at an open-air drama played by actors--except that it was all too real.

# Disaster

The platoon kept on moving in short stops and starts. Finally, they reached the bridge and crossed into the friendly perimeter. There the road turned to the southwest running between the shoreline and a narrow gage railroad. The area was a picture of a disaster. Bodies of Chinese soldiers were scattered over the landscape, as well as U.S. dead and wounded. Vehicles were parked at all angles, and all types of equipment and supplies littered the terrain. Rifles and automatic weapons fired intermittently throughout the perimeter. Periodically, one of the tracked vehicles would commence firing with a spectacular display. Toward the west end of the area, several 105mm howitzers were emplaced. They fired at any target presenting itself, including groups of individuals. Squads of enemy infantry could be seen massing for the attack. As the platoon began trooping into the perimeter, the black war birds of the Marine Air Wings began circling overhead. Periodically a single aircraft would peel out of the formation and streak to the attack. A black and orange mushroom marked the point of impact of a napalm drop. Second Lieutenant John W. Schneidermann gazed across the breadth of the American position: the hill mass to the south, the reservoir to the west, the inlet to the north, the valley of the Pungnyuri-gang to the east, a bowl with the enemy looking into it. "Like shooting fish in a barrel," he thought. In his mind, he pictured a great ancient army, the rear guard of Charlemagne, King of the Franks, as it fought in the wild passes of the Pyrenees: the armored men and horses, arrows in flight, the bright waving banners, the tragic figure of Roland defending to the last against overwhelming odds.

Reality appeared in the form of a company headquarters messenger. "Sir, the CO sent me to guide your platoon to their positions."

"Oh, yes, thank you, Soldier. We'll go up to the head of the platoon and check in with the platoon sergeant," the lieutenant answered. The two soldiers jogged forward to where the platoon sergeant was sitting along the roadside. The lieutenant spoke up, "Sergeant, this man is from the company and will take us to our positions."

The sergeant looked up. "Well, lead on, Soldier."

Keeping low and well dispersed, the platoon scrambled to the south edge of the perimeter, the portion of the line that faced the high ground. The new position had been organized and constructed by the riflemen of the 3rd Battalion of the 31st Infantry. These individuals had been under siege for the last two nights. They had come close to being overrun but, with the aid of their artillery, had beaten off the quilted legions of the People's Liberation Army. The platoon leader dispersed the squads in the same order as in the old emplacements. The platoon sergeant located a CP bunker near the firing line, but it was far inferior to the one which they had just abandoned. The men settled down to make the best of their situation.

Second Lieutenant John W. Schneidermann moved from squad to squad, checking with each man and each squad leader. "Sergeant Martin, how are you doing?"

The young sergeant replied in a low, serious voice, "I'm down to five men counting myself. Are we going to get out of here, Lieutenant? I have never seen anything like this, Sir!" The young non-com was definitely rattled, his words pouring out incoherently.

The platoon leader looked the man squarely in the eye. "Where are you from, Sergeant?"

"I'm from Ohio," the young sergeant answered. The young man then described in great detail a modest middle-class home and family, caring parents, and a respectable home life.

The platoon leader listened carefully, and when the distraught soldier finished, he spoke in a slow, measured tone. "Let me tell you something, Sergeant. I am depending on you to take care of this squad. Your dad would tell you the same thing if he were here. Now I know things don't look great, but we are going to win. You have done a good job so far. You keep up the good work because I am proud of you. Now you get your men ready to hold this line."

The young non-com looked up with a glint of determination in his eyes, "I'll try, Sir," he said in a low voice.

"That's the spirit, Sergeant," the lieutenant replied as he gave the young soldier a light slap on the shoulder.

The machine gun squad was set up and ready to fire. The platoon leader inquired, "How are the guns, Sergeant Cobb?"

"Just fine, Suh. Ah seen some chinks up on the hill. Do ah have permission to fire?" the squad leader asked.

"I would suggest that we be careful about giving away our automatic weapons positions until we are attacked," the lieutenant observed.

"I understand, Suh. Ah am goin' to find more ammo with your permission, Suh," the squad leader stated.

"By all means, Sergeant Cobb."

Second Lieutenant John Schneidermann walked over to the new CP bunker. The command group was assembled and busily getting set up. The runner, Polowski, was checking the phone while the rest of the crew was tidying up.

"This bunker is a pig pen, Lieutenant!" Sergeant Pratt exclaimed. "As a matter of fact, this whole perimeter is a disaster. We could build a bunker out of dead chinks. I've never seen so many."

The platoon leader faced the command group and announced, "OK, men, let's get this outfit shaped up. Sergeant Ridehout, you work on the ammunition situation. Sergeant Pratt, you take Garza and check the men for frostbite problems. Tell the squad leaders to pull a foot inspection. Try and make sure the men have dry socks. Let me know if you have any problems. Polowski, call the company and see what the ration story is," the lieutenant continued. The platoon leader took Sergeant Pratt aside as he left the hunker, "Keep your eye on Martin. I'm worried about him."

Second Lieutenant John W. Schneidermann sat in the bunker, trying to mentally sort out the present state of affairs. He thought: *What is really going to happen? You have to take stock of your assets and look at your liabilities.* In spite of the harrowing events of the past days, John Schneidermann felt a certain air of confidence. He had passed the test to the satisfaction of his severest critic--himself. He had stood up to the rigors of combat and had come through a winner. He thought: *There is always that question: Will I stand up, or am I a coward? Show the white feather, as they say in old England. Well, here we are defending this godforsaken piece of frozen real estate that wouldn't raise enough to feed a goat. It's kind of ridiculous if you get right down to it. Here I am, a greenhorn second john leading an under-strength bunch of scared kids. Well, nothing to do but keep going.*

Second Lieutenant John W. Schneidermann walked up to the 2nd Squad position. The men were busily hacking at the frozen ground with their entrenching tools, those versatile, tough little folding shovels, the true infantryman's friend. "How's it going, Sergeant?" the lieutenant inquired.

Sergeant DiAngelo looked up through the wool scarf wrapped around the lower part of his face. "About as well as can be expected, Lieutenant. What's going to happen now?"

The platoon leader replied, "The orders are to hold this position."

The young sergeant continued in a low monotone, "It looks like the 31st just about lost it."

71

"It does look that way, all right. How are your men holding up?" the lieutenant asked.

"They are hanging in there," was the quiet reply.

"I know it's been tough, Sergeant, and you have been doing a great job. If we can hold out, the situation should get better," the platoon leader stated as he tried to put on an optimistic face.

The lieutenant moved to the right flank squad and approached the squad leader. The men of the squad were performing the usual tasks required in a new set of entrenchments: checking equipment, tending small fires, and hacking at the frozen earth that formed the floor of the trenches and foxholes. The ground was hard with frost for the first few inches, but below that, the digging was comparatively easy.

A shroud of apathy seemed to have settled over the squad. The platoon leader walked up to the squad leader, "How is it going, Sergeant?"

"Not worth a damn, Lieutenant. This place is a graveyard."

"It's depressing all right, but we have to look on the bright side," the platoon leader responded.

"And what might that be, Sir?" There was a tone of sarcasm in the young non-com's voice.

The lieutenant spoke with an air of confidence, "We are still on our feet and fighting, O'Malley, and that's the main thing."

The sergeant replied sullenly, "Yeah, but for how long? We are in this icebox with the whole chink army on top of us. It looks like it's a matter of time until they wipe us out."

The platoon leader spoke sternly, "Look, Sergeant, I don't like this any better than you do, but we can't give up. If we do that, we are licked. Now I know it looks bad, but if we all hang in there, it should get better. You have done a good job. You have fought a tough enemy and come out on top. Don't quit now."

The young soldier replied, "I guess you are right, Sir."

The platoon leader lightly punched the sergeant on the shoulder. Second Lieutenant John Schneidermann walked slowly back to the platoon CP bunker. The runner was sitting beside the small gas stove, which was burning with a bright blue flame. On the little stove was a tin can partly full of boiling water. In the can were several cans of C-Rations. "The rations should be done in a minute, Sir. There's one in there for you."

"Thanks, Polowski." The platoon leader sat down heavily, took off his helmet, and took a deep breath.

72

The runner spoke up, "Would you like ham and lima beans, Sir?"

"That would be fine, Polowski."

The runner fished out a can from the boiling water with a wire hook. "Here you are, Sir. Could I open it?"

"That would be fine, Polowski."

The runner held the hot ration can with a gloved hand and cut out the top with a C-Ration can opener. The lieutenant's thoughts drifted away from the cold, harsh reality of the bleak surroundings.

# On Leave

"You know that there is going to be an old-fashioned barn dance this Saturday, John," Mrs. Schneidermann remarked as she looked up from the newspaper. She was a trim woman in her late forties with an air of sophistication about her.

"Where is it going to be?" John asked.

"At the big barn on the Miller place," his mother answered.

"I remember that barn. It's really a classic--must be the biggest barn in the county. Who's putting it on?" John continued.

"It's that dance club. You know, it's a club that anyone in the county can belong to. You should think about going, John. I know that most of your friends are out of the area," the mother remarked.

"Did you know that barn has a hardwood floor? It makes a good place to have a dance. There must have been a lot of money in that farm when it was built. One thing about a barn dance is that you can wear your old clothes," John Schneidermann said with a grin.

The crowd began gathering quickly. It was an ideal evening for early fall--clear, cool, with a crisp northwest wind. The barn could have been on a page of the Farm Journal. It was an imposing structure, straight and trim with white siding. Built on a hillside with the second floor at ground level, the lower part was essentially a walk-out to the cattle yard. The foundation had been constructed from split field stones, and the upper part of the wood frame with the joints was put together with wooden pegs. Although the building hadn't been used for housing livestock for several years, it had been kept in excellent condition.

The dance club had decorated the inside of the barn with great imagination. There were paper streamers, pictures on the wall, extra lights of various colors, and bales of new hay placed around the edge for seating. The atmosphere was indeed festive. Soon the band began to tune up, and strains from the fiddles pierced the air. A table covered with a checkered cloth held ice-cold cider. John Schneidermann strolled through the crowd stopping at the table selling tickets. "This looks like a big event," he remarked.

"That it is," replied a plump woman of thirty, a member of the club. "This is our major fundraiser for the year. We are glad you came."

The crowd was colorful--the women in bright, checkered, long dresses and the men in jeans, plaid shirts, and neckerchiefs. John ambled over to the cider table as the announcer started talking

74

over the microphone. "We are glad to see you all here tonight. There's going to be a great program. In the best tradition of the dance club, we are going to have something that will appeal to the beginner and the expert, starting in about ten minutes."

The cold cider tasted good. A few of the rougher members of the crowd added to the cider from pocket flasks. An overweight deputy sheriff in uniform stood near the entrance creating the appearance of order. It was a congenial crowd, and while later in the evening, there could be disturbances, at the start of the program, all was serene. The brightly colored dancers began to move out onto the floor, the music started up, and the program began. The caller spelled out the movements to give the novice dancers a chance to join in. It was a lively event.

John Schneidermann joined in several of the opening sets--old favorites like the Virginia Reel. Taking a short break, he headed back to the cider table. Sipping on a cup of the amber liquid, John gazed at the animated scene.

"You're John Schneidermann, aren't you?" The voice belonged to the girl standing beside him.

John turned to face a tall, slim, fair-haired young lady in a light blue, checkered gown.

"Yes, I am. How did you know?"

"I met you at the speech contest, you know, the final event at St. Paul," the girl answered.

"Oh, yes, I remember, but you look different," John responded.

"Well, that was years ago," the girl remarked with a smile.

"Your name is--let's see--don't tell me, ah--Louise--um--Nelson?"

"Yes, that's right," she crisply replied.

"You're from St. Paul, right?" John Schneidermann conjectured.

"Yes, but I am visiting my cousin who lives in this area," Louise said.

The meeting seemed to be predestined. The two young people danced to the "Tennessee Waltz" and other lilting, sentimental melodies. The night slipped by. Oblivious to their surroundings, the young couple sat in a corner talking.

"What are you doing these days, John?"

John Schneidermann answered, "I am in the Army. I'm home on leave."

"When do you have to go back?" Louise asked.

"I'm leaving Wednesday for Korea." A long silence. John finally spoke up, "What are you doing tomorrow? Why don't I stop by?  We could… there are several things we could… why don't I come by in the morning?"

"That would be fine, John," Louise replied with a slight smile.

The evening festivities continued toward midnight.

John thought happily: *This is really a fantastic program. It's amazing what a friendly crowd there is here. Everyone is congenial and witty. This punch is exceptionally tasty. It's amazing how well the band has been playing, and the setting and the decorations, they are incredible. It's remarkable meeting Louise after all this time. It had to be a coincidence, but what a stroke of good fortune. This really did turn out to be a great evening!*

In what seemed like a few minutes, the evening drew to a close. The final number had been played, and the dancers began filing out. "Can I offer you a ride, Louise?" John asked.

"I really feel that I should go with the people I came with, but why don't you come by tomorrow?" the slender girl replied.

"I guess I don't know where you are staying," the young farmer blurted out.

"Well, let me write it down." The tall, pretty girl in blue took out a pencil and wrote the directions and a telephone number.

"What would you think about coming over for dinner--or church--we go to the country church. Ten-thirty?" John asked.

"That sounds fine to me, John, if it would be acceptable to your mother," the slim girl stated.

"Oh, Mom will be glad to have you come for dinner. She's a great cook. I could call her right now," John spoke up.

"No, not at this hour, but I will be happy to go with you to church and home for dinner," Louise said firmly. John walked her over to where her cousin was standing. Louise made the introductions. The cousin was a stocky girl with rather coarse features. She was most cordial, grabbing John's hand and pumping it up and down.

"John, this is my cousin, Dorothy Nelson. Dorothy, this is John Schneidermann, an old friend from the speech contest."

Dorothy burbled spontaneously, "It's so nice to meet you, John."

The young soldier took Louise by the hand, gave it a gentle squeeze, and said haltingly, "I'll see you tomorrow."

"I shall be looking forward to seeing you again," she said with a shy smile.

With that, the farmer's son turned and lightly walked out of the open door of the big barn and over to his parked car. Thoughts passed through his mind like frames from an old-time silent movie. *What an amazing coincidence. It's funny. I don't remember her from the contest. I wonder what her situation is. Do you suppose she's already engaged? No, it can't be. She wouldn't be this friendly--or would she? I can hardly wait until tomorrow. I'll have to talk to Mom about dinner.*

The drive home was short. John parked the car and bounded up the back steps of the farmhouse. As he turned on the kitchen light, suddenly he was overcome by hunger. He opened the door to the white refrigerator, taking out some milk and two slices of ham. With some homemade bread, mayonnaise, butter, and lettuce, he concocted a sandwich. He turned and saw the figure of his mother in the doorway. Mrs. Schneidermann was wearing a light blue terrycloth robe. She spoke in a calm, quiet voice, "Did you have a nice time, John? I have been worried that you haven't had much fun on your leave."

The young soldier looked up at his mother. "Oh, I had a great time. As a matter of fact, I wanted to talk to you. You see, I met this friend, ah, from the speech contest, and I was wondering if this friend could come over for dinner tomorrow."

"That would be just fine, John. What do you think we should have for the main course?"

"How about some of that good roast beef? Is there any more of that left in the freezer?" John inquired.

"I'll take a package out now. Tell me about your friend. What's her name?" his mother queried.

"I didn't say it was a "her," John replied.

"You didn't have to, Son."

Second Lieutenant John W. Schneidermann spent the night tossing and turning. In the morning, he rolled out at the first trace of daylight. He thought: *It's amazing how things can change in one day. That dance last night, was it a dream? No, it was real. I better get up and get going. It's important to make a good impression.*

John began digging out his dress uniform from the closet. "I didn't think I would wear this for a while," he thought. The uniform was new, and it fit well. It was a set of "pinks and greens," a dark, olive-green blouse, wool worsted trousers (grey with a pink tinge), brown shoes, a tan shirt, and a dark green tie. John went down to the laundry room and set up the ironing board. Getting out a well-used iron, a pressing cloth, and a spray bottle containing water, he began to eliminate any traces of wrinkles in the uniform.

The figure of his mother appeared in the doorway. "You better let me finish that for you, John."

The young lieutenant turned the pressing over to the skilled hand of his mother and began concentrating on polishing shoes and brass insignia. The U.S. crossed rifles and gold bars took on a high shine from the effect of the cloth of jeweler's rouge. In a few minutes, all was done, with the final product hanging on a hanger in the doorway.

"I think it looks very nice, John," his mother remarked with a certain air of pride.

"Thanks a lot, Mother. You have the professional touch," the young soldier said with a look of gratitude.

She returned to the kitchen and started breakfast. John walked into the kitchen where his father was sitting at the table. He spoke up in a pleasant voice, "Sit up and have some oatmeal, Son." The young man took his place at the table. After a few moments of silence, the father spoke up, "I hear you met this great girl, Son."

John looked up with a grin. "Well, that could be, Dad, but you never can tell."

"Yes, I know how unpredictable some women can be," the father teased. Mrs. Schneidermann frowned at her husband.

John replied, "Seriously, she does look pretty sharp, but you will be able to see for yourself. I am planning on picking her up for church."

The breakfast was a typical country-style meal with cooked cereal, toast, coffee, pancakes, and all the other incidentals, such as jelly and butter. "Good breakfast, Mother." John jumped up. "I better get going."

The sunshine was spilling into the farmyard. The air was clear and cool, an ideal fall day on the Northern Plains. The farmyard was typical, with a large, two-story house, a barn, and assorted outbuildings.

The car was a 1940 Ford V-8, a black coupe with a lot of chrome. It was in good condition and had plush upholstery and a radio. John quickly put on his work clothes and, with a bucket of soapy water, began washing the car. Because it was fairly clean, the washing didn't take long. After a rinse, he wiped the surface off with a chamois skin. With a small whisk broom, he brushed out the inside.

John Schneidermann walked briskly into the house, well-satisfied with the appearance of the gleaming vehicle. "Give them any color they want just so it's black," was what Henry Ford supposedly said.

After a quick shower and shave, the young officer put on his freshly pressed outfit. It showed the results of the professional tailoring job.

"You look elegant, John," his mother said with a soft smile.

"Thank you," the young officer replied as he planted a quick kiss on his mother's cheek. He did indeed look the part.

"We want to be sure and get some pictures, John."

"OK, Mom." Second Lieutenant John W. Schneidermann climbed into the sporty black Ford and started down the road. He attempted to avoid as much dust as possible. After about a fifteen-mile trip, he pulled into a farmstead. The building site was a bit on the cluttered side, with farm machinery parked at random and a liberal collection of junk equipment in view. The house was small and in need of paint. The young lieutenant parked by the entrance to the house yard, a gate in a woven wire fence erected to keep the chickens out. John stepped lightly along the walk and knocked at the well-used back door. The cousin, Dorothy, answered the knock and greeted the visitor with a friendly smile. "Come on in, John. Louise will be here in a minute," she said pleasantly. John was led into the living room and directed to a large, well-worn leather chair. The room had the same cluttered appearance as the farmyard, with a liberal number of family pictures on an old upright piano, many potted plants of all descriptions, and an excess of antique furniture. Dorothy took a seat across from the newcomer and sat on the edge of her chair. She began rattling a steady stream of comments, all of which passed over John Schneidermann without his comprehension. Suddenly from the stairway leading to the second floor, Louise appeared. She was wearing a trim grey suit with a white blouse, white gloves, and a stylish hat. The sight almost caused the young farmer's jaw to drop. This was one sharp-looking young lady. She had looked quite attractive in a blue-checkered, old-time gown, but this attire was spectacular. All the slim lines that were hidden before were now emphasized.

John Schneidermann stood up somewhat awkwardly and spoke quietly. "Good morning, Louise. You certainly look nice."

"Why, thank you, John. I could say the same about you," she replied with a smile.

Dorothy seemed delighted. "Let me get a picture," she said as she rummaged in the drawer of a large antique bureau. The couple stood together as Dorothy snapped several poses. Louise was attractive, polished, and sophisticated, of which she was well-aware. She was prepared to make a favorable impression on the people she would meet today.

The couple said goodbye and walked briskly out to the parked car. John opened the door on the rider's side, and Louise gingerly stepped in. John walked around the car, opened the door, and slid behind the wheel. "This is a very attractive car, John, so neat and clean," Louise smiled brightly.

"Thank you. It has been a good car," John answered. They rode along the country road, inhaling the beauty of the fall season.

"It is so thoughtful of you to invite me, John, or should I say, Lieutenant?"

"It's my pleasure, Louise, and you don't have to use any title."

The sun was shining, and the temperature was cool but not uncomfortably so. Soon, in the distance, a church spire appeared. As the car came closer, the entire building came into view. "Oh, what a delightful church, John! It is so beautiful with the pine trees!" Louise exclaimed.

"Glad you like it, Louise," John replied. The little black Ford pulled into the parking lot. John stopped, got out, opened the right-hand door, and waited as Louise carefully stepped out. "This is such a lovely setting, John. I am so glad to be able to attend the service," Louise spoke as she looked at the peaceful setting. The young couple climbed the seven steps to the large, arched doorway. Louise took the arm of her escort as she reached the head of the stairs. After taking a bulletin from an usher, they walked up the right aisle to a place about halfway to the front. All eyes were on the pair, especially on the attractive, tall girl no one knew.

The service went by in a flash: the scripture readings, the hymns, the sermon. At the end, all arose and drifted toward the back of the church, where the pastor was extending a friendly greeting. John made several introductions as he and Louise made their way toward the open doorway. Louise was most gracious as she threaded her way through the crowd of unfamiliar faces. She had the ability to remember names, a skill she now applied seriously. The crowd was spilling into the front yard amid a volume of friendly chatter. Louise was her charming self as people came by for an introduction and a brief chat. John was amazed at the way in which this newcomer made herself a part of the group. "So nice to have met you, Mrs. Schmidt. What a lovely church and such a striking setting."

After a few minutes, John's parents walked up, and their son made the introduction. Louise was at her public-relations best. "I am delighted to meet you. I think I would have recognized you. There is such a striking resemblance to John. I do hope that my coming won't be an inconvenience."

Mrs. Schneidermann grasped the extended, gloved hand and replied, "We are happy to meet you, Louise, and it's no trouble at all having you." The parents were obviously impressed with the polished and talented young lady. "Well, we will see you in a few minutes," the mother smiled as she spoke.

John had been feeling about ten feet tall since picking up Louise this morning. There had been an amazing transformation from the country dancer to the sleek, urbane woman. The two young people climbed back into the little coupe and started down the gravel road.

"Those people are so charming and friendly, John. How far is it to your home farm?"

"Oh, about five miles. We'll be there in a few minutes." The car rolled along between two fields of standing corn, the loose, tan leaves flapping in the gentle breeze. In the space of ten minutes, the sporty black Ford turned into the driveway. "Here we are, Louise, the old homestead," John announced with a grin. They got out of the car, walked up the narrow concrete sidewalk, and climbed the steps and into an enclosed front porch. The big two-story house had a well-furnished living room. The dining room adjoined through an oak archway. Both rooms had oak wainscoting on the lower three feet of the walls.

As John and Louise walked into the living room, John's mother met them with a pleasant greeting. "Louise, come right in. Please sit right over here." She gestured toward an attractive sofa.

"Oh, thank you. What a lovely room. I can't help admiring that paneling," Louise replied. "Is there anything I can help you with, Mrs. Schneidermann?"

"No, thank you, dear. Just be seated and relax for a few minutes," the mother answered pleasantly. Mrs. Schneidermann had set an elegant table with sterling silver, china, and a fine linen tablecloth that had been in the family for several generations. Relishes, jellies, homemade bread, and pickles in ornate dishes, in addition to the centerpiece of flowers, decked the table.

"You may all sit up to the table," Mrs. Schneidermann announced as she stepped into the living room. "Louise, you may sit here; John's over here." Her husband went to his usual place at the head of the table while his wife took a place nearest the kitchen. After a table prayer by the lady of the house, the meal began. The food was delicious, as was always the case when Mrs. Schneidermann cooked. There was tender roast beef, mashed potatoes and gravy, a salad, corn, and a glazed sweet potato dish.

"My, this is such a wonderful, tasty meal. I feel honored to be invited," Louise commented pleasantly.

"Thank you, dear. We are delighted that you could come," the mother replied.

The conversation turned to the church service. Louise recited in detail all the people she had met and some facts about each one. John thought: *How could she have remembered all those names and information? That is amazing... she must have a photographic memory.* In reality, she had trained herself to become proficient in memorizing names and facts.

Louise turned to John's father and said charmingly, "Tell me, Mr. Schneidermann, in your opinion, what is the economic effect of tile drainage on crop production?" August H. Schneidermann sat in a sort of stunned silence.

At last, he replied, "Well, we have done some tiling, and it worked pretty well. As far as the dollars go, it looks like a good investment."

Louise smiled in a knowing sort of way, "I am not an expert on the subject, of course. I read an article on drainage recently, and I thought it was most interesting."

John thought as he looked at Louise, *Is there anything that she doesn't know something about?*

Dessert was a piece of cherry pie, a specialty of the cook. "This was a sensational meal, Mrs. Schneidermann," Louise exclaimed. "Everything was just delicious. Now I insist on helping you with the dishes if I may borrow an apron." Louise smiled as she spoke. The two women disappeared into the kitchen, chatting as if they had been friends for years. John and his father moved back into the living room.

"That is some girlfriend you have there, John," his dad commented.

"I guess you're right," John replied in a rather subdued voice.

82

In the kitchen, the dishwashers were making rapid progress. Louise worked with deft efficiency. "I am so impressed with your home, Mrs. Schneidermann. Everything seems to be so properly done."

"Oh my, no, dear. We just have a few simple furnishings. When we finish, let me show you around."

Louise was something of a romantic but with a practical side. She could see the rich, black soil and the well-kept fields. She could also see that she was making a favorable impression on John Schneidermann. In her mind's eye was a picture of blue-eyed children with the handsome features of the farmer's son.

John's mother took some time and showed Louise the main parts of the house. At last, they were back in the living room. The girl in the trim grey dress had created a dazzling image for the young prairie soldier. All sense of normalcy and practicality had faded from his consciousness. The whole scene was incredible. Everything seemed to be so perfect, so correct. Second Lieutenant John W. Schneidermann sat in a warm, happy daze, content just to listen to the bright conversation.

# Assault

The hot can of ham and lima beans tasted incredibly good. "How about a cracker or two to go with that, Lieutenant?" the runner asked.

"That sounds good, Polowski."

The two senior sergeants, Pratt and Ridehout, approached from the direction of the company CP. They climbed into the trench and sat down. The platoon sergeant, with some effort, recovered two cans of hot C-Rations from the boiling water.

The platoon leader turned to the two sergeants. "I have been talking to the squad leaders, and they are all down in the dumps. I can't say that I blame them, but it's no time to give up." The lieutenant continued, "It's obvious that we are surrounded by a powerful enemy force. We have to hold on. There is just no other choice. Do either of you have any ideas?" The two men were silent.

The platoon sergeant finally spoke up. "I think we are all worried, but you are right about not giving up." The men stared at the ground.

The platoon leader spoke up again. "The platoon has done a good job, and we just have to keep it up. I want the boys to know that this is one platoon that is going to make it! We are going to get out of this rat trap if it's the last thing we do. Now let's get down to business. Ridehout, how is the ammunition situation?"

The sergeant answered, "Every rifleman has at least 200 rounds, and the ARs have their magazines full. The machine guns have six boxes each, and Cobb is out scrounging for more. Each man has at least six grenades."

Second Lieutenant John W. Schneidermann continued the discussion with the two sergeants. "The ammunition supply looks good. Now I want all the weapons in the rifle squads inspected. Sergeant Pratt, you take the 1st Squad, Sergeant Ridehout, you take the 3rd, and I'll take the 2nd. Make sure all the chambers have been cleaned, and make sure all the excess oil has been wiped off. If you find a serious problem, such as a weapon that won't fire, automatic or semi-automatic, let me know. I think we can find some weapons that will work if we have to. Now let's see if we can get everyone to start looking on the bright side."

The three men moved up to the firing line. The lieutenant and Sergeant DiAngelo met at the squad position. "How are the weapons in your squad?" the platoon leader inquired.

"They have been working OK as far as I know," the sergeant replied. "Let's make a quick check."

The two men moved rapidly down the squad line. "How is your weapon, Soldier?"

"Not too bad, Lieutenant, except once in a while, I have to work the bolt by hand."

The platoon leader took the rifle, pulled back the bolt, and looked in carefully. "Do some cleaning on this weapon. The operating rod end, the part that slides in the gas cylinder, is probably worn. I'll see if there is a better rifle around. Remember that your rifle may be the only thing between you and the chinks. Are you able to keep your feet warm?"

"Well, most of the time, Lieutenant. I have been trying to keep an extra pair of socks under my jacket."

It sounds like you're doing things right," the lieutenant stated. "Did you get your rations heated?"

The soldier looked up with a sheepish grin. "Yeah, but I burned the beans."

The sun had come out sometime during the day, but as the afternoon wore on, it began to dip toward the western hills. The men of the platoon kept busy throughout the day, improving their positions and servicing their weapons and equipment. Pushed on by the exhortations of the platoon leader, they kept at their tasks doggedly until the daylight faded.

"The lieutenant sure is getting picky. You'd think we were back in Japan on Saturday morning inspection."

"He might be a little green, but he's right about the weapons. And I'll say one thing for sure-- he sure turned out to be one hell of a fighting man."

The perimeter was occupied by the two infantry battalions, and the artillery was about a mile east to west and a half mile north to south. The perimeter was manned by both battalions. The much-reduced 3rd Battalion, 31st Infantry, held the east side while the 1st Battalion, 32nd Infantry, held the south side facing Hills 1459 and 1250, the west side, which was up against the reservoir, and the north side, which was along the inlet. The artillery was drawn up inside the perimeter, with the tracks spaced around the 105 howitzers. The picture resembled the famous British square that had supposedly never been broken despite the words of Kipling's poem.

During the day, the runner had laid separate phone lines to the 81st mortar platoon and the 60th mortar section.

The platoon leader had walked to the mortar positions and obtained a sheet of prearranged concentrations. The concentrations were designated by numbers that corresponded to specific points on the ground. A front-line observer could call for a concentration by number, and the mortars would immediately send a flight of projectiles toward the target.

Around the middle of the afternoon, several cargo planes came over and dropped supplies. The men of the platoon looked up to see the strings of multiple parachutes as they floated down. Not all the drops landed within the perimeter. After a while, a lone helicopter swooped into the area like an oversized dragonfly. The men of the platoon observed the chopper as two casualties were loaded, one on each side. The whirling craft returned a short time later to fly out two more wounded men.

As the final rays of the sun receded behind the mountains, the men of the platoon braced for another desperate fight. After some time, the moon appeared, casting a pale light over the broken landscape. The temperature dropped, heading into the below-zero range. The men of the platoon anticipated a major attack as soon as the darkness fell, but no attack developed. This night the line was on full alert. The men had an opportunity to get some much-needed rest during the day and were ready. The prodding of the platoon leader had produced results. The men, although cold and demoralized, had responded with diligent preparation for the action that would most certainly come. Making a last-minute check of the line before the light failed, the platoon leader made a few last-minute adjustments.

The firearms of the infantry platoon, principally the M-1 rifle, the Browning Automatic Rifle, and the light machine gun, all fired the same cartridge, the 30-06. This powerful round could punch a jacketed bullet through a two-foot tree. At the machine gun position, the squad leader had been working hard to put it into the best possible condition. The guns were placed in such a location that they could each sweep the platoon front. The emplacements were extended and deepened, and boxes of ammunition were piled by each gun. Sergeant Cobb, the squad leader, was everywhere, bringing up extra ammunition, digging in the tripods, sighting the guns, and always cleaning the two weapons. The guns were the light of the sergeant's life. He was constantly lavishing attention on the two A4 lights and was always looking for any technology that would improve their performance.

The platoon leader moved up to a position slightly to the rear of the machine guns at a point where he could observe the guns and the entire platoon line. Along with the runner and his phone

86

line, he prepared for the coming night's action. The platoon sergeant moved up with the left flank squad and the assistant platoon sergeant, the right flank squad. The moon became brighter, but as time went by, clouds drifted in, and it started to snow. All was quiet except for the distant sound of artillery to the west.

The machine gun squad leader was at the left handgun emplacement, searching the front with his field glasses. The platoon leader crawled over to join him. "Anything out there, Sergeant Cobb?"

"Not a sign of any movement, Suh."

"Are you all set on the guns?" the lieutenant asked.

"Yes, Suh, we are all set to be able to hit about anything on the platoon front; I checked each gun myself," the sergeant reported. The gun crews were sitting silently beside their weapons. The guns themselves, almost like living things, inert, motionless, sat ready to spring to life on command. The guns were sitting on the parapet immediately on the forward edge of the trench. A perforated steel jacket encased the barrels of the weapons to provide a cooling effect when sustained firing produced excessive heat. The butt end of the gun was like a box with a pistol grip projecting out with a single trigger. The top of the receiver had a cover that unlatched at the back and hinged at the front. To load the gun, the cover was opened, a belt laid on the open receiver, the cover closed, and the operating handle pulled back and released. This was the half-load position. One more pull of the operating handle and the weapon was ready to fire.

The snow continued to sift down over the platoon position as the night vigil continued. No enemy activity could be heard or seen anywhere along the infantry line. The men had expected the worst, and an air of tension had permeated the foxholes and trenches. When nothing happened, they began to relax and doze off. The platoon leader and the machine gun leader continued to search the platoon front with their glasses.

Sometime around midnight, the sergeant gripped the platoon leader's arm. Silently he pointed to a movement to the right front of the line. The lieutenant nodded in response. The lieutenant whispered, "I'm going to try to get some mortar fire." John Schneidermann slid back to his position and the phone.

" Mortar platoon," came the reply to his low whistle.

"Fire concentrations 15, 16, and 17." In a few seconds, there was the thump of the 81 mortar rounds leaving the tubes. In a high arc, the shells passed over the heads of the men on the line and landed on their targets. That prompted a flurry of activity all along the platoon front. The lieutenant now called for mortar fire on all the concentrations. In a matter of seconds, the terrain in front of the riflemen erupted in what seemed like a continuous, rolling series of explosions. The bugle calls of the enemy infantry could be heard above the detonating shells giving an eerie unreality to the scene. The infantrymen now opened fire all along the line. In a burst of action, pushed by pent-up anger and fear, the men laid down an awesome sheet of high-velocity fire. Any movement, any shadow, drew the lethal, smashing bullets of the U.S. Infantry line. It was again a case of determined riflemen fighting from behind a defensive position facing an equally determined attacker. All the frustration and misery of the past few days came to the surface. The men were firing in a wild, unrestrained manner, with instinct taking control of their actions.

The machine gun crews had held their fire. Ready and waiting, the gunners crouched behind their weapons. The machine gun squad leader held his position intently, staring at the unfolding drama of the enemy assault. When it seemed that the clamor of the firing had reached a crescendo and that the attackers were gaining momentum, the gun squad went into action. On a prearranged signal, the left handgun started sending a stream of deadly slugs at the dodging, moving, ever-advancing shadow figures. The gun made a sweep of the front concentrating on any suspected target. The gun was firing short bursts allowing the weapon to maintain a continuous stream of fire. The instant the first belt was expended, and the gun was reloading, the right-hand gun opened fire. The sheer volume of fire from the platoon was too much for even the dedicated, tenacious, peasant soldiers of China. That, along with the well-placed mortar fire, stopped the assault before it could gain the necessary momentum to over-run the U.S. line. After another halfhearted attempt at breaking the platoon's hold on the line, the enemy backed down.

During the rest of the night, several attacks were mounted against other segments of the perimeter. These, too, were beaten off with the aid of supporting weapons. The mortars, the 105s, and the AAA guns all joined in to produce a symphony of battle sounds. The flashes of weapons and overhead flares illuminated a desperate combat scene. Toward morning the fighting started to wind down, and the men of the platoon could look forward to the next day. Morning light came slowly to the perimeter, delayed by ground fog. By midmorning, however, the fog had broken. The men of the platoon slowly crawled from their entrenchments, relieved to have survived another night of desperate combat. They had come through but at a cost--four fatalities and several wounded.

Garza, the platoon medic, had worked frantically to treat the casualties as they occurred. The hardest hit was the First Squad, where two men lay dead, one the squad leader, Sergeant Martin. The platoon leader organized a litter party that moved the fallen to a designated location near the aid station. The lifeless forms of the soldiers lay side-by-side in a row. They all seemed so peaceful now, at rest, out of reach of the freezing cold and the flying steel. The lieutenant stood for a moment, looking down at the men who, only a short time ago, had been vital, vibrant members of the unit. Their faces seemed serene, mask-like, but there was no time for sentiment, no time for ceremony. The business at hand was survival. The men of the platoon set about taking care of the routine tasks--cooking rations, cleaning weapons, and drying socks.

To the south of the firing line rose a massive hill crowned by a peak designated as 1456 on the map. The slopes of the hill were partially covered with snow which outlined the draws and ridges. The peak was about three-fourths of a mile from the platoon line and about 1200 feet higher. Enemy riflemen could be observed on the high ground in small groups, but little firing took place. As soon as the weather permitted, the Marine Corsairs returned to the skies over the perimeter. They dove into the attack, targeting groups of enemy soldiers or any other quarry that would present itself. In the afternoon, another airdrop was made to the ragged defenders. The men of the platoon again watched as the parachutes drifted down.

Second Lieutenant John W. Schneidermann called the two senior sergeants to the platoon CP to discuss the events of the past night and the prospects for the coming hours of darkness. The lieutenant spoke in a tired voice, "What happened to Martin?"

The platoon sergeant was staring at the ground. He finally answered, "A rifle bullet, I guess. They didn't get close enough for grenades."

"How many able bodies have we got left?" the lieutenant inquired.

The platoon sergeant thought for an awkward length of time, finally saying, "About twenty as near as I can tell."

Silence.

The platoon leader continued, "All the boys did a great job last night. I don't think the chink attack got off the ground. I wonder how many we got?"

Sergeant Ridehout answered, "There must be at least fifty out there."

"Any wounded?" the lieutenant wondered.

"There might have been, but they all froze," the sergeant replied.

The platoon leader continued, "We better break up Martin's squad and put his men in the other squads."

The lieutenant spoke in a slow, quiet voice, "Sergeant Ridehout, you see about ammunition. Sergeant Pratt, let's check the line."

The platoon sergeant's voice wavered as he spoke. "Do you think there will be a relief column today? Man, I'm really beat. I don't know how long I can keep this up."

The young officer replied, "I don't know about the relief, but I do know that the Division CO flew in today. That would sure seem like a good sign. Well, at least the chink attack last night wasn't as bad as the other two nights. Maybe they are backing off."

"I sure hope so," the sergeant responded in a trailing voice. The platoon leader headed for the line, followed by Sergeant Pratt. Thoughts crowded the lieutenant's mind: *We came through another night. I'm worried about the platoon sergeant. He's acting like he's losing his grip. What do you do about that? I hated to lose all these men. Was there something that could have been done differently? I don't think there is going to be a relief column. This damn cold weather! I'll say one thing. The platoon fought like tigers. This whole thing is unreal.*

"How are you doing, Soldier?"

"Could be worse, Lieutenant."

"You fought like a pro last night. The chink attack never got to first base. Let me see that rifle." The platoon leader opened the bolt of the weapon and looked it over in detail. "That weapon looks like you've got it in fine shape. Keep up the good work."

"Lieutenant?"

"What is it?"

"I heard that there is a tank battalion coming in today. Is that true?"

"I haven't heard that, but I hope it's so."

The platoon leader moved along the line, checking rifles, asking questions, and complementing the men. The platoon sergeant followed along, saying little, looking at the ground. At the machine gun position, the crews were busily working on the weapons.

"Well, Sergeant Cobb, how are you this afternoon?"

"Just fine, Suh. We are almost ready to go."

"You and your men did an incredible job. Without your guns, we wouldn't have held. Keep up the good work."

"Thank you, Suh."

Second Lieutenant John W. Schneidermann slowly walked back to the platoon CP. He slid into the crude bunker and slumped into a corner.

Polowski, the runner, was boiling water over the little gas stove. "I'll throw a ration in for you, Sir," the runner said with a slight smile.

"That would be fine, Polowski.". The young officer set his rifle against the dirt wall of the bunker and leaned back. He sat motionless, staring at the wall. His whole system seemed to shift to neutral.

# Mistakes

John Schneidermann was part of the crew, and he was proud of it. The high point of the farm year was harvesting the yellow gold of the Minnesota prairies. All through the summer, the green corn rows had grown under the energy-giving sun and had swelled from the life-giving rains. It was time to bring in the harvest. The stalks stood in silent rows, clad in their tan garments. John, for his youth, was a capable hand. He had learned the trade from the ground up. The mission now was to move through the fields with a two-row mounted picker. This model set on an International M tractor gathered up the corn stalks, stripped off the yellow ears, and elevated them into a trailing wagon. The picker, operated by one man, moved up and down the field. The work was demanding. It was always a race against time when the sky turned grey, and the snow would come, signaling the end of all work in the field.

The Schneidermann operation involved two pickers, two plowing units, and two men hauling the picked corn. It was taken to the farmstead, where it was elevated into round cribs formed from rolls of snow fence. John was one of the haulers. He would start from the field with a loaded wagon pulled by a smaller tractor, drive down the road about two miles and turn in at the farmyard. He would then pull across the end of the sloping elevator that was set over the filling crib. Moving the wagon to the correct position, John would pull down the apron of the elevator directly across the end of the box. He would start the tractor that operated the elevator and open the end gate of the wagon. As the corn ears poured from the box, the young farmer would start the wagon tractor and raise the wagon box. When the box emptied, John would lower the hoist, raise the apron, and take off for the field with the empty unit.

It took a coordinated effort to keep the operation rolling. Weather was the god that ruled all the harvests. Rain and wind could stop the best efforts of men and machines. There were broken chains, ruptured hoses, flat tires, and dead batteries, all obstacles to the timely completion of the work.

John Schneidermann felt a glow of pride as he wheeled the empty wagon into the cornfield. His dad, operating the red tractor and the mounted picker, was waiting. John pulled up behind the picker and unhitched the empty wagon. In a few minutes, the two wagons were switched and ready to go.

The man on the picker climbed off and walked over to where his son was standing. "How's it going, John?"

"OK, Dad."

"Be careful with these loaded wagons. They're heavy, you know."

"I will, Dad."

The young man rolled out of the field at a fast clip. As the tractor moved down the road, heat from the engine was channeled back to the driver through a canvas shroud, the popular "Heat Houser." John Schneidermann felt a surge of pride as the tractor rolled down the gravel road, "Not many 14-year-old guys could handle this job," he thought to himself.

Several minutes later, the tractor approached the farmstead entrance. The entrance was narrow, and the side slopes of the embankment, steep. As John began slowing up to make the turn, his foot moved forward to the brake pedal. On the red, International tractor, there was a brake for each of the large rear wheels. To properly engage the brakes to slow the machine smoothly, both pedals should be locked together as recommended in the operator's manual. As the young driver hit the brakes, his foot slipped and pushed in only the left pedal. With incredible swiftness, the tractor made a jackknife turn and plowed into the ditch. The tractor went in front end first, with the loaded wagon right behind. When the machine landed in the ditch bottom, it rolled on its side, taking the wagon with it. There was a splash of ear corn, a crashing of metal on metal, and a final thump as both rigs made their final landing. John was thrown clear, landing in a heap on the ditch bank. He sat up, dazed and shaken, looking at the wreck in disbelief. It seemed to John Schneidermann that his dad arrived at the scene in an amazingly short time. The farmer pulled up in his pickup, screeched to a stop, and ran to the site of the accident. "Are you hurt, John?" he yelled in a loud voice.

"I guess I'm OK," John answered.

"What happened?" his dad asked hoarsely. A long silence.

"I guess I was going too fast. I'm really sorry, Dad." A powerful sense of guilt overtook the farmer's son.

Two of the other men arrived, and with the use of a log chain and tractor, they pulled the disabled equipment out of the ditch. The damage was comparatively minor, and they soon had the battered tractor running. With sledgehammers and jacks, they straightened the wagon tongue. The three men with scoop shovels soon had the spilled corn reloaded. As the men finished the cleanup, August Schneidermann spoke up, "Thanks, men, let's get back to work." As the men moved off to their respective tasks, they gave John a reassuring nod and a light punch on the shoulder.

When the farmer finished looking over the damaged tractor, he turned to his son and said in a quiet, firm voice, "Well, John, at least nobody was hurt. Let's get back to work. Remember, Son, we all make mistakes, and we all have setbacks, but we don't give up."

# Desolation

Toward the middle of the afternoon, the men of the platoon began preparing for another night in their positions. Rumors and talk of a coming rescue effort circulated. As was typical of army rumors, they grew with each telling: "Airborne troops were going to drop into the perimeter…. The Marines were moving up from the south…. The 17th Infantry was on the way supported by tanks." But as the daylight faded and no reinforcements appeared, the men of the platoon realized they were on their own. They were manning essentially the same positions as they did the previous night but with fewer people. The men were wearing down both physically and mentally.

The enemy started attacking early in the evening with mortar fire. Behind the exploding shells, the enemy infantry began closing on the U.S. lines. The Chinese assaults were hitting all portions of the perimeter, looking for weak spots, and appearing to concentrate on three distinct points. Fortunately for the men of the platoon, they held one of the stronger segments of the line. All through the night, the battle continued building to a new level of ferocity. It appeared that the Chinese were making an all-out effort to overrun the perimeter. The supporting weapon continued to maintain fire, but now the diminished ammunition supply was becoming a concern. The platoon had taken several enemy mortar rounds early in the night but, because of their improved positions, had suffered no casualties. Two weak demonstrations against the platoon line by the enemy were beaten off.

Second Lieutenant John W. Schneidermann was moving along the line, keeping low, stopping at each position. Only two rifle squads remained, one on the left, and one on the right, with the machine guns in the center. The continued cold and the light snow were adding to the already depressing situation.

At the left flank squad, the lieutenant questioned Sergeant DiAngelo, the squad leader, "Where's Sergeant Pratt?"

"I don't know, Lieutenant. He just left about a half hour ago. Didn't say a word to me." A long silence.

"How is your ammunition supply?"

"It's OK for now," the squad leader replied wearily.

The two men crouched in the trench, staring forward. The sounds of battle echoed from the other sides of the defensive perimeter. The platoon leader gave the young sergeant a meaningful slap on the back as he crawled out of the trench. The young officer kept moving, climbing into each position, giving a word of encouragement, and asking a vital question. The men were drifting into a kind of stupor, a sort of mental twilight where there were only a few basic elements: life, food, sleep, warmth, and honor.

The platoon leader made his way back to the CP. The runner, Polowski, was wedged in the corner of the bunker, phone in hand. "The CO wants to talk to you, Lieutenant."

The young officer picked up the handset and gave a low whistle.

"CP," was the answer on the wire.

"This is Schneidermann. Is the CO there?"

"Hang on." In about one minute, the CO came on the line, "How are you making it, John?" The voice was low and halting.

"We are hanging in there, but the men are wearing down."

The CO continued, "Hold on, John, you're doing a good job."

The lieutenant asked, "How are things with the rest of the perimeter?"

After a long pause, the CO replied, "It doesn't look good. There have been some breakthroughs, and the ammunition for the quads and the 40s is running low. I don't know if we can take another night of this. Several hundred wounded are at the aid station, and the supplies are running out. There is no way to evacuate them." A long silence. The CO continued in a low, hoarse voice, "Keep up the good work, John. Keep in contact."

"Yes, Sir." Second Lieutenant John W. Schneidermann slumped down against the cold wall of the bunker. Thoughts flitted through his consciousness: I *wonder what became of Pratt... Man, am I getting tired... The CO didn't sound good... The men are really performing. I wonder for how long? I'm not sure we can hold out... This is a crazy situation... Here we are in this remote part of Asia, trying to fight off these Chinese hordes. This is like Gunga Din... I wonder what Louise is doing. It would be great to see her again.*

PFC Elmer C. Polowski broke the spell. "Is there anything you need, Sir?"

"Ah, no. Nothing. Thanks, Polowski. I've got to get going."

"I made a cup of hot chocolate. Would you like some, Sir?" the runner asked.

"Oh, you know, I would at that," the platoon leader answered. The young officer took a long drink of the steaming liquid. That's really good. I appreciate that. How did you make it?" he asked.

"Well, I started up the stove and used some C-Ration cocoa," the runner replied. "How are things going, Sir?"

"We are still holding, but this is the worst night so far, according to the CO," the lieutenant answered.

"I heard from the company that the chinks broke through the east side," the runner stated. "It sounds like they are attacking all around the perimeter."

The platoon leader spoke again, "Did you see Sergeant Pratt?"

"No, Sir. He hasn't been here at the CP."

Second Lieutenant John W. Schneidermann left the bunker and slipped up to the firing line. The riflemen gave the appearance of being under a hypnotic spell. They moved more like robots than living beings. They were still on their feet despite the fatigue, the gnawing hunger, and the penetrating cold. Any movement to the front drew their fire, and the hint of amassed enemy incited a flurry of automatic fire from the ARs and the light .30s. Despite his own exhaustion, the platoon leader felt a surge of pride. His men were still fighting, still holding on in the best tradition of the U.S. Infantry. The night hours seemed to drag by endlessly, but finally, the light started breaking through the eastern skies. Scattered enemy fire kept up even as the daylight strengthened, and bullets were still passing through the perimeter. That the Chinese controlled the high ground all around the task force worked to their distinct advantage. They could observe the entire perimeter from those commanding heights.

Daylight revealed a scene of desolation. Overcast skies and light snow completed the disheartening picture. The platoon leader was in the right flank squad area sitting next to Sergeant Ridehout. "Have you seen Sergeant Pratt?"

"No, Sir, I haven't seen him all night."

The runner, Polowski, approached the two men, "I heard that we are going to pull out of here today."

"Who told you that?" the sergeant asked.

"The company clerk said he heard it from battalion," the runner responded.

The lieutenant spoke in a subdued voice, "That is some news. You haven't seen anything of the platoon sergeant, have you?" The runner silently shook his head.

The platoon leader spoke again, "Polowski, will you see if you can find the Sergeant? And watch your step. We're still drawing some rifle fire." The lieutenant turned to Sergeant Ridehout. "How are you holding up, Sergeant?"

"Well, this has been a tough deal, Sir, but I think I can keep going for a while," he answered.

Both men sat silently staring at their grim surroundings--the snow-streaked earth of the emplacements, the discarded cartons and cases, and communication wire weaving patterns across the broken landscape. The platoon leader spoke in a calm, considered voice. "I really appreciate all your efforts. You have been a real leader."

The sound of scattered shooting could be heard as the two men sat staring over the firing line. The platoon leader suddenly straightened up. "We better get going, Sergeant. You check on ammunition, and I'll man the CP. Send the squad leaders over one at a time."

"Yes, Sir."

The lieutenant trudged to the CP bunker. The platoon medic, Garza, was manning the phone. The usual clutter of equipment and weapons lay around the interior of the bunker. In a few minutes, Sergeant O'Malley, the 3rd Squad leader, ducked into the crude structure. The young sergeant slumped into a corner without a word of greeting. His face was drawn and haggard. He gazed out of red-rimmed eyes. The soldier wore the hood of his parka under his helmet, and a rifle cartridge belt with a bayonet and accessories.

The lieutenant spoke, "How is your squad?"

After a lengthy silence, the sergeant began speaking in a low monotone. "Johnson got hit and went back to the aid station. I think he will be back. That leaves four, including me. One of the ARs is giving some trouble. The men are really beat. I don't know how long they can keep going. What are we going to do, Lieutenant?"

"Let me say first that you and your squad have done a remarkable job. Few could have performed as you did. I wish I could tell you what's going to happen, but I don't know. Polowski heard a rumor that we are going to pull out today, but that's only a rumor." The lieutenant paused. "I would like to have you go back to the squad and get ready to move if we get the order."

The squad leader stared at the floor of the bunker in silence. Finally, he spoke. "OK, Lieutenant. I guess I better get going."

As the 3rd Squad leader crawled out of the bunker to start back toward the firing line, the weapons squad leader, Cobb, stepped into the bunker. "Morning, Suh," the sergeant spoke with an air of formality.

"Good morning, Sergeant. How do things look at the machine gun position?"

"Pretty good, Suh. We did quite a lot of shooting last night, and we're getting ready to go again."

"What's the strength of your squad?"

The young non-com immediately replied, "Six counting me and one ROK, Suh." Sergeant Cobb wore a field jacket, a finger-length coat with large pockets, as an outside garment. When worn over several layers of clothing, it made a very serviceable winter garment. He carried a rifle and wore a .45 automatic pistol on his right hip in a regulation, covered, leather holster.

"You and your men did an incredible job last night. We couldn't have made it without you."

"Thank you, Suh."

"We don't know what's going to happen today, so get your squad ready for any eventuality. Polowski heard a rumor that we are going to break out today, but it's just a rumor. How much ammunition can your squad carry on the march?"

"Well, I would say six boxes for each gun, Suh."

"That seems like a heavy load for the men, including the gun and tripod," the platoon leader said in quiet response.

"It is, Suh, but we can do it," the sergeant replied.

"Have you seen the platoon sergeant?" the lieutenant inquired.

"No, Suh, I haven't seen him all night," the sergeant replied.

"Well, that's all I had in mind. Keep up the good work," the lieutenant said in a low voice.

"Yes, Suh." The machine gun sergeant climbed out of the bunker and ambled back to the firing line.

A short time later, the 2nd Squad leader, DiAngelo, poked his head into the shallow bunker.

"Come on in, Sergeant. I wanted to talk with each squad leader and see how things look from your point of view," the lieutenant stated. The young non-com sat down on the bare dirt floor and set his rifle and helmet in one corner of the crude shelter. "You haven't seen Sergeant Pratt?" the officer asked.

"Not since I saw you last, Lieutenant." The effects of the night's fighting were etched on the young soldier's face. He sat for about a minute in silence.

The platoon medic, Garza, spoke up, "They want you on the phone, Lieutenant."

The platoon leader picked up the handset and spoke, "This is Schneidermann."

The voice of the first sergeant came through the speaker, "The CO wants to see you in fifteen minutes."

"OK, I'll be there." The lieutenant turned to the squad leader and spoke, "I have to report to the company CP. I wanted to ask you what condition your squad is in. Polowski heard a rumor that we were going to break out today, but it's only a rumor. I'll try to find out about it at the company. You and your squad did a tremendous job last night. No one could have done better," the platoon leader stated in a firm voice.

The squad leader looked up with an empty stare. "I don't know if we can take another night. It looks to me like the whole damn chink army is out there. The more of them we shoot, the more that keep on coming. If we don't get some kind of break, I don't think we are going to make it. The cold's getting unbearable."

The young officer replied in a steady voice, "I know it looks tough, Sergeant, but we have to keep on trying. We just don't have any choice. Now you go back to your squad and look after your men. They need you. I have a lot of confidence in you. We all need you." The platoon leader started to leave, looked back at the sergeant, and grinned, "Come on, DiAngelo, I know you can do it."

A weak smile showed on the squad leader's face, "I'll try, Lieutenant."

"That's the spirit. I'll see you later." The platoon leader headed for the company CP at a brisk jog, keeping low and glancing over his shoulder from time to time. The company command post was located within a hundred yards of the platoon positions. It was set up in a shallow trench covered with a large tarp. Inside was the company command group and two of the platoon leaders. The company commander, a young first lieutenant, had been in command for only three days. The

100

men were gathered around a battered field desk and an EE8 hand-crank telephone. The faces of the group were grim. The fourth platoon leader joined the gathering.

# Breakout

The company commander held a lighted cigarette between his right thumb and forefinger with the lighted end under his palm. He was nervously taking quick pulls on the cigarette. The first lieutenant spoke in a low, steady voice, "We are going to break out of this encirclement starting at 1200 hours."

The decision to attempt to break out of the perimeter was made in desperation. The task force, named for its commander, Lieutenant Colonel Don C. Faith, had been cut off and surrounded for three days and four nights. They had been under almost continuous night attack by at least one PLA division. The task force, which was down to less than 2000 able-bodied men, was attempting to break out of the grip of about 10,000 tough, hardy, peasant Chinese soldiers. The U.S. force was about ten miles from the town of Hagaru-ri, the advanced base of the 1st Marine Division. The infantry and artillery soldiers who made up the task force were worn down by the vicious fighting and the debilitating cold and snow. There were serious shortages of ammunition, medical supplies, and gasoline. The presence of over 500 wounded men was a severe drag on Task Force Faith. One high card held by the Americans was the supporting Marine tactical aircraft. The 7th Infantry soldiers had moved up along the east side of the reservoir with an easy victory in sight. They became strung out along the narrow dirt track that followed the shore of the Chosin.

Out of the vast expanse of Asia came these disciplined, tenacious, relentless soldiers in their quilted uniforms and with their bugles. They had isolated the U.S. forces into segments in a single coordinated night attack. The segments had joined, and now they had to run the gauntlet. The gauntlet consisted of a frozen track surrounded by ominous hills on the one hand and the ice-covered reservoir on the other. Little help was available save the black Marine Corsairs as the Marine regiments to the south fought for their lives. It was run the gauntlet and live, or stand and fight and die. Time was running out as the Marines at Hagaru-ri planned to withdraw to the sea within the space of a few short days. The company commander continued, "Our mission will be to guard the trucks. We will cover the east flank of the convoy and keep the enemy off the column. We will stay as far out as possible. C Company will take the point. The 3rd Battalion, 31st will be the rear guard. As soon as the weather clears, Marine air will support us. All the artillery, mortars, and excess vehicles will be destroyed. Any questions?"

All the officers remained silent, each with his own thoughts. The company commander continued. "The 3rd Platoon will take the company advance guard. Now go back to your units and report back as soon as you are ready to roll. With a few breaks, we'll be in Hagaru-ri tonight."

The platoon leaders scattered, heading for their outfits. The platoon runner, PFC Polowski, met the lieutenant as he left the company CP. "I found Sergeant Pratt," he reported.

"Where is he?"

"I better show you, Sir," the runner replied. He led the way to a point inside the perimeter about 100 yards east of the company CP. In an unkempt field lay the body of the platoon sergeant. The two soldiers stared at the still body sprawled face down on the snow-covered ground.

"I wonder what he was doing here," mused the lieutenant.

"It looks like he was hit by a stray bullet, Sir. There are no other marks on him."

The lieutenant thought for a moment: *Why had the platoon sergeant left the line during an attack? Where was he going? He had been depressed, no doubt about it.... What should I have done differently? Pratt was an experienced combat soldier.... I sure hate to lose him! But we can't help him now. We must get going. It's a good thing we are breaking out.*

"Should we carry him to the aid station, Sir?"

"We don't have time, Polowski. Take his weapon and ammo." The platoon leader, followed by the runner, threaded his way back to the platoon CP. The sky was still overcast but was showing signs of clearing. The two men broke into a run as they crossed the snow-covered field through clumps of grass and amid the debris of battle.

At the platoon CP, which appeared as a low hump on the surface of the drab landscape, Sergeant Ridehout was manning the phone.

The platoon leader stepped into the CP trench and turned to the runner, "Get the squad leaders here on the double!"

The sergeant was heating a tin can of water over the single burner stove. The steam was rising from the boiling water forming clouds of vapor as it hit the cold air. "Sergeant Ridehout, you are now the platoon sergeant. Sergeant Pratt was killed last night."

The sergeant turned with a perplexed look. "What happened, Sir?"

"We just don't know. We found him east of the company CP. It looked like he was hit by a stray bullet."

"What was he doing back there?" the sergeant asked.

"I guess we'll never know."

The squad leaders came at a run. The prospect of moving was an invigorating tonic to the dejected men. They piled into the narrow bunker. Lieutenant John Schneidermann fired out orders. "Polowski's rumor turned out to be true. We're breaking out at 1200 hours. The company has the mission of protecting the left flank of the truck column. We will be the lead platoon. The first objective is to take the high ground to the east. The Marine air will be here as soon as the sky clears. We will keep together with the 2nd Squad in the lead, then the machine guns, and then the 3rd Squad in the rear. Anything we can't carry, we should destroy. That won't be much except for a few rifles. Bring anything extra to the CP, and we'll take care of it. I'll stay with the machine guns and Sergeant Ridehout will march with the 3rd Squad. If all goes well, we'll be in Hagaru-ri before nightfall," the lieutenant stated emphatically. "Any questions?"

"What about any wounded?" asked one of the non-coms.

"We will move any wounded to the trucks," the platoon leader answered. "One more thing. Sergeant Ridehout is now the platoon sergeant. Sergeant Pratt was killed last night."

The faces of the men showed renewed hope--the vision of safety, warmth, hot food, and sleep played in the minds of the young non-coms.

"Report when you are ready to go," the platoon leader ordered. The squad leaders abruptly left the bunker and headed back to the firing line.

The runner came up to the CP carrying three rifles. "These are extras, Sir."

"Take them apart and scatter the parts around. I hate to do that, but there is no other way." The platoon leader gathered his kit together in preparation to leave: pack, sleeping bag, field glasses, map case, and rifle.

Sergeant Ridehout spoke up, "Would you care for a can of hot rations?"

"That would be great. What have you got?"

"Beans and franks, I think," the sergeant replied. The sergeant fished out an olive-drab can and juggled it from glove to glove, finally passing it to the lieutenant.

The young officer opened the can with a familiar C-Ration can opener. The hot beans were incredibly tasty. "Man, are these beans good! Did you have some for yourself?" the lieutenant asked.

"Yeah, I had some before," the sergeant responded.

The platoon leader turned to his new top sergeant and asked, "What are your thoughts on the breakout?"

After reflecting for a few moments, the sergeant replied, "The thing I am worried about is running out of daylight. If we lose air support, we could be in trouble. I hate to think about it. We just have to be optimistic."

The runner poked his head into the bunker. "The squads are ready to go, Sir."

"OK, tell them to stand by," the lieutenant answered as he grabbed the phone. Responding to the whistle, "This is Schneidermann. We are ready to go."

"Good. We will give you the word, Lieutenant. It looks more like 1245, though."

"OK, Sergeant. We'll be waiting for the word." The leader stooped over and made his way to the doorway of the bunker. "I'll walk the line. Stay on the phone."

The artillery and heavy mortars were firing rapidly, expending the last of their ammunition. The enemy, observing from the high ground, could see the preparations for movement. They began increasing their mortar fire on the perimeter. Amid the increased noise and confusion, the sky began showing increased signs of clearing. Second Lieutenant John Schneidermann could feel his spirits rising. As he stood in the CP trench surveying the landscape, thoughts crowded into his consciousness: *If we can just make it out of this trap.... The men are feeling better.... If the Marine air can make it.... Ten miles isn't far.... Should be able to march ten miles in four hours.... This whole battle is unreal.... Those damn chink mortars—where did they get all that mortar ammunition? How many enemy riflemen are out there anyway?*

The platoon leader moved to the firing line, stooping as he walked. He dropped into the left flank position. Two men were sitting on the edge of the short trench. The trench was about three feet deep, with a parapet built of the excavated dirt. One man was armed with a Browning Automatic Rifle, and the other an M-1. "How's it going, men?"

"Well, it's so far, so good, Lieutenant. We'll feel a lot better if we get the hell out of here," the AR man replied. "Are we really leaving, Lieutenant?" the rifleman asked.

"That we are, and it won't be too long now, as soon as the Corsairs get here," the young officer responded with enthusiasm. "How are your feet?"

"They are good enough to walk out of here, Lieutenant."

105

"That's the spirit, men. I'll see you on the road." The young officer moved from hole to hole, talking to the men in the squads. There seemed to be a revived spirit on the platoon line. The men were eager to be on the move.

"I'm ready to go right now, Lieutenant. Just give us the word."

At the right flank squad, the platoon leader noticed that each man had a box or two of machine gun ammunition in addition to his normal gear. "What's the deal here?" he asked, pointing at the boxes.

A rifleman replied, "Cobb talked us into it. He said he needed that much ammo to keep off the chinks."

The young lieutenant made his way back to the CP. "Anything happening?"

The runner, the medic, and the platoon sergeant were holding down the CP bunker. "Nothing new, Lieutenant," the runner commented.

"It looks like the squads are ready to move out," the platoon leader stated. "Are we all ready to go here?" he asked.

The platoon sergeant answered, "We are about as ready as we'll ever be." He continued, "We got rid of all the surplus weapons and equipment, Polowski is going to take the phones, and Garza will take the stove."

The four men sat in a tight circle in eager anticipation of the order to start moving. Waiting has been a part of warfare since the dawn of time, and this was no exception. There is always hope for better times when soldiers are waiting for something to happen. The reverse is true when a campaign bogs down, and there is no end in sight. The battered remnants of the platoon could now see action coming, and, with action, the hope of an escape from the death grip they were locked in.

A whistle on the phone signaled an incoming call. The platoon leader picked up the handset. "3rd Platoon."

The company commander spoke in a tense voice, "Time to move out. We're closing up shop."

"Roger. We're on the way," the lieutenant answered, and then turning to the other occupants of the bunker, called out in a loud voice, "Let's roll."

106

The four men briskly moved out of the CP bunker for the last time. The platoon leader signaled with an upraised right arm, and the platoon swung into action. Sergeant DiAngelo had his squad on their feet and moving out. The machine gun squad followed with their guns and equipment on their backs and over their shoulders. The rear of the platoon file was brought up by the 3rd Squad, with the platoon sergeant the last man in line.

It was about a half mile from the platoon positions west to the road. The high ground to the southeast was dominated by Hill 1250. The platoon, strung out in single file, was following the toe of the mountain in a generally southeast direction. The platoon leader could see activity to the west along the road. Trucks were moving into line in an effort to form a column of vehicles. Suddenly, a flight of four Corsairs came into view. The gull-winged planes circled briefly, and then without warning, one craft peeled off and swooped down on the road just ahead of the column. The first fighter was followed one at a time by the other three in what apparently were dry runs. The first plane circled again and then dived at the breakout point. This time a napalm tank tumbled from the belly of the aircraft. As the plane pulled out of its maneuver, a black-fringed, orange burst shot up, marking the point of impact of the fiery missile.

The platoon was now making good progress, skirting the high ground east of the road. A narrow-gauge railroad ran parallel to it. The rough terrain and the snow underfoot made the going arduous for the heavily loaded infantrymen.

On the high ground to the left and to the front of the platoon, the Marine aircraft were making repeated runs on the dug-in enemy. With rockets, 20mm automatic cannons, and napalm, they were hitting the enemy infantry with devastating effect. As the enemy soldiers abandoned their positions for safer ground, the relentless aerial attackers wreaked havoc on the exposed troops. The young office from the Northern Plains could see the form of a hawk as it hovered over the prairie and then suddenly dove on its prey.

The platoon kept moving forward, meeting limited opposition. They continued to skirt the hill mass, and where it approached the reservoir, they turned south along the railroad. The task force was rolling. The continuous assaults by the Marine aircraft, which were striking within a few yards of the U.S. infantry, had demoralized the enemy.

As the Chinese soldiers fled over the ridge lines, the task force kept moving down the road. The platoon drifted across the railroad and down to the road. They were behind the lead company and ahead of the trucks. The men were moving in single file on the left shoulder of the road at intervals of several yards. Second Lieutenant John W. Schneidermann kept the platoon together in its original formation: an understrength rifle squad in the lead, the two machine gun crews next, and a reduced rifle squad bringing up the rear. The platoon leader moved up and down the line while maintaining a critical eye on the entire formation. As the men tramped along, the lieutenant could sense their morale rising. Their faces reflected confidence or perhaps even optimism.

The road ran in a southerly direction from the point where the task force had broken out of the perimeter. It followed the shoreline of the reservoir for nearly two miles. On the far side of the railroad, which ran beside the road, the hills rose upward to the east. Thus, the task force was moving south with a rifle company in the lead, the trucks following, infantry alongside, and an infantry rear guard. An M-19 twin 40-tracked vehicle led the trucks. Two M-16 quad .50s were in the convoy.

The platoon leader signaled a halt. The men moved to the ditch for cover. Because they had been moving since the breakout began, the break was welcome. Some lit a cigarette, some just slumped down, some were talking.

The lieutenant walked along the road to the rear of the file. He was looking up at the snow-covered hills looming to the east. Some long-range enemy rifle fire was coming from that direction. It was not having any effect on the men on the road. The machine gun squad leader, Sergeant Cobb, threw a gun into action and started firing at suspected targets.

The platoon leader thought as he walked along the line: *The men are sure looking great. Things are going good.... If we can just keep rolling.... I wish we could somehow move faster.... Even the cold doesn't feel so bad.* The faces of the men passed by as if in review with a variety of expressions on the weathered countenances of the young infantrymen: impassive stares, looks of concern, questioning glances, slight grins, a thoughtful gaze.

The young officer from the Northern Plains looked into the eyes of the men as he passed. For a brief second, as their eyes met, they would seem to silently say, "For a new officer, you're not too bad. You have done a good job of leading the platoon. We think that you are a real soldier. We hope that you can get us out of this miserable predicament."

The point man of the lead squad, Ferguson, was playing his harmonica. The strains of "Gary Owen" drifted along the platoon line. "Hey, Ferguson, do you want to know what you can do with that mouth organ?"

"Yer problem, Mon, is that you no understand good music."

The platoon sergeant, Ridehout, was on the road scanning the hills to the east. As the lieutenant approached, he turned and asked, "How do things look up ahead?"

"The lead company has stopped, but I don't hear much firing," the lieutenant replied calmly. "How are the men holding up back there?"

"Well, we are moving. So far, so good. Everyone is anxious to keep moving," the sergeant answered.

Second Lieutenant John W. Schneidermann turned and started walking down the road toward the head of the file. As he neared the lead squad, he signaled the men to move out with a downward sweep of his raised right arm. The riflemen, with some effort, awkwardly rose to their feet and started down the road. After some time, the platoon approached the rear elements of the lead company. Beyond the lead company, the land opened to the east in a wide valley. An inlet stream flowed down the valley from the east into the reservoir. The road crossed the inlet stream on a short, single-span, concrete bridge. After crossing the stream, the road turned to the east and climbed over a saddle east of Hill 1221. The railroad turned and followed the shoreline of the reservoir. The platoon leader, closely followed by the runner, bounded ahead to a point immediately south of the bridge.

When seen up close, it was obvious that the span had been demolished, apparently by enemy explosives. This was an unexpected threat to the continued, southward movement of the truck column. Everything depended on keeping the task force moving and making it to the protection of the Marine division before darkness set in.

The forward company was now filing around the wrecked bridge and across the frozen creek bed. They were continuing up the road heading toward the ridge line. In increasing numbers, the enemy could be seen up the valley to the east, ahead on the crest of Hill 1221, and on the hill northeast of the demolished bridge. The enemy appeared to have built a roadblock at the point where the road climbed over the saddle on the ridge.

Fire from the enemy infantry was beginning to build up, striking the area around the destroyed bridge and on the troops that were moving up the road to the south. The platoon now crossed the frozen stream and followed the trailing elements of the lead company. As the platoon reached a position partway up from the bridge on the road toward the roadblock, they stopped, unable to proceed. The lead company stopped ahead of them, apparently obstructed by intense fire from the area of the roadblock. The platoon moved off the road and into the right road ditch.

The lieutenant looked back at the bridge and at the trucks trying to cross the valley. The tracked M-19 was towing the vehicles through the rough, frozen stream bed. Time was slipping by, and daylight was beginning to fade as the task force desperately tried to regain its momentum. The Marine Corsairs were making a valiant effort to protect the soldiers of the task force from the encircling enemy. Despite their best efforts, however, the enemy fire kept increasing. The platoon held its position, trying to keep low to avoid the small arms and automatic weapons fire that kept splattering around them. The men of the platoon could see that events were turning against them. The cold was omnipresent, and fatigue was setting in. Casualties mounted as the enemy fire took effect. Daylight was fading as the Marine fighters made their last attacks on the advancing enemy.

Second Lieutenant John W. Schneidermann was having difficulty maintaining control. He knew that some of the men had been hit along the road but not exactly how many. It was obvious that the task force was rapidly disintegrating into isolated groups. The success of the breakout hinged on being able to cover the distance to Hagaru-ri during daylight hours. Once the truck convoy was stopped by the blown bridge, the entire operation was in serious jeopardy. The enemy was closing in rapidly from three directions.

The platoon continued to lie in the frozen ditch, trying to survive, wondering what was in store as the day drew to a close. What had begun as a promising run to the safety of friendly lines had now degenerated into a holocaust of death and destruction. The tough, tenacious, disciplined soldiers of the 80th Division of the People's Liberation Army had triumphed over the mechanized, modern soldiers of the 7th Infantry Division of the United States Army and their black, death-dealing war birds.

The young officer from the Northern Plains was now crouched in an icy ditch in a faraway part of the frozen mountains of Asia. Thoughts were racing through his mind: *What went wrong? This thing is turning into a total disaster. What should I do now?*

# What's Inside

The inside of the big shop had the appearance of a cave. Everything was dark, the ceiling and the walls and all the tools and machinery, covered with dirt and grime from the coal smoke. Two arched wooden doors large enough to drive in a vehicle through were always open during warm weather. A diverse assortment of tools filled most of the shop: grinders, a trip hammer, a drill press, and other similar devices. There was a row of power tools that were driven from an overhead jackshaft.

At one end of the building, like an ancient altar, was a large forge. The coals glowed, and a wisp of smoke drifted up from the bed of the forge. Two large anvils stood nearby, mounted on massive blocks of timber. Hanging on the walls were other props of the blacksmith's trade: hammers, chisels, punches…. On one wall was a streaked calendar with a picture of a racehorse.

Presiding over the dingy surroundings like a medieval priest in greasy bib overalls was the blacksmith, Oskar Reinhardt. Oskar was a large, stocky man in his sixties, a German immigrant, and a master metal worker.

John Schneidermann drove up to the shop in the old 1932 Model B Ford truck. He parked the truck, got out, and walked into the shop carrying the two pieces of a broken steel shaft. Oskar tilted up his welding helmet and looked up from a glowing piece of red-hot steel.

"So, Johann, the son of the big farmer, comes to see old Oskar. You know how to farm, but you still need the old blacksmith to do the tough jobs," Oskar said with a wicked-sounding laugh.

John grinned as he displayed the two pieces of the broken shaft. "Dad thought you could weld this. It will take more than a week to get a new one."

"Ja, I see what you got there, Johann. Lay it up on the bench."

John put the two broken pieces of the twisted steel shaft on the cluttered welding bench. Oskar dropped his helmet and resumed welding. John looked away from the dazzling arc as it played on the red-hot steel. Oskar finally raised his helmet, revealing a dirt-streaked face and glasses etched by numerous chips from the electric welder. Oskar walked to the bench and looked at the broken shaft. "I knew your great grandfather, Johann. Did you know that?" The blacksmith spoke with a distinct accent.

"I guess I didn't know that," replied the seventeen-year-old.

Oskar picked up the two pieces and walked to the grinder. Soon a shower of sparks came from the spinning stone. "You have to know what's inside the steel to know how to weld it. Did you know that, Johann?"

"That sounds right to me," answered the lad.

The blacksmith beveled the edges of the steel where the break had occurred. "Ja, I show you, Johann. You can tell a lot by watching the sparks." Oskar put the metal to the grinder again and watched as the sparks showered to the floor. "You see, the sparks tell you what the steel is made of. Your great-grandfather helped me get started in the blacksmith business when I came to this country. I teach you these things, Johann. Then you will know how to be a blacksmith." Oskar laughed at the thought. "But you don't want to be a blacksmith, Johann, when you are the son of the big farmer."

John stood silently, listening to the blacksmith ramble on. Oskar Reinhardt was born in Mecklenburg in what is now Germany, in the early 1890s, the son of a blacksmith. He had learned the trade well and was recognized as a dean of his vocation. In 1914 he was conscripted into the Imperial German Army. He served through four, long, bitter years where he had seen great and terrible things. He left Germany in 1919, settling in the Western Minnesota town where he served the farmers of the area.

Oskar fastened the broken pieces of steel to the bench with four, large clamps. He went to a battered wooden cabinet and, after a brief deliberation, selected several welding rods. Oskar snapped the ground clamp to a leg of the welding table and turned on the electric welder with the flip of a large switch. The electric arc lit up the area around the table. With a practiced hand, the master iron worker guided the rod along the break. Oskar turned the round steel shaft as he continued the welding process. John stood by, watching the work but avoiding a direct view of the bright arc. After a few minutes, Oskar removed his helmet and shut off the large, boxlike welder. "We let it cool and then a little grinding, and then we are done, Johann," Oskar solemnly stated.

"What made that thing break in the first place?" the young man asked.

"There was a flaw in the way it was made, a mistake at the mill," answered the blacksmith. "I'll show you something, Johann." Oskar walked over to a well-used desk, opened a drawer, and removed a large knife. The knife was a product of Oskar's master hand. It was a beautiful piece of craftsmanship with brass and silver on the handle. "What do you think of it, Johann?"

John looked at the knife with interest. "It looks really nice."

"Now, I show you something else, Johann." Oskar took the knife over to one of the anvils. He took a 3/8-inch bolt from a pile of iron and placed it on the anvil, set the knife on the bolt, and struck it with a hammer, slicing the bolt in two.

"That's really some knife, Mr. Reinhardt!" John exclaimed.

Oskar laughed uproariously, "You like it, Johann, and it is 'Mr. Reinhardt'? The son of the big landlord calls the old blacksmith "Mister." John laughed along with Oskar. "Ja, we are all equal here in America, and you and I are old friends."

After they both recovered their composure, John asked in a serious voice, "How did you make a knife that will cut through a bolt?"

"It's the steel, Johann. It's what's inside the steel."

"You look at a piece of steel, and how do you know what is inside or what it can do?"

"You know from the sparks, Johann. From the sparks, you know how to tell the right kind of steel," Oskar said in a serious voice. "Men are like steel, Johann. It's what's on the inside that makes the man. I learned that in the German Army, Johann. I saw many men. Some were weak, and some were strong, just like the steel.

Oskar took the welded shaft and shuffled over to the grinder. After starting the abrasive wheel, he expertly placed the red part up to the stone. The sparks flew in a shower as Oskar put a finishing touch on the welded shaft. Your part is ready, Johann," the blacksmith announced.

"It looks like a good job, Oskar," John observed.

"Ja, every job that old Oskar does is a good job. I am the master of the iron, Johann. Here, you keep the knife."

John was delighted with the wonderful gift. "Thanks a million, Oskar. I really like it!"

"Ja, you're a good boy, Johann. You've got good steel."

# Do or Die

Bullets were hitting the road embankment and the ground above the ditch. Every now and then, one would strike the frozen surface of the road and ricochet off with a whining sound. The men of the platoon pressed themselves tighter into the ditch in an effort to escape the increasing enemy fire.

Second Lieutenant John W. Schneidermann was stretched out on the rough ground trying to make sense of a chaotic situation. Thoughts, like photographic images on a rapidly changing screen, were flashing through his mind: W*e are in one hell of a mess.... Amazing how quickly things changed. Here we are with no supporting weapons whatsoever, strictly man to man and outnumbered ten to one.... The big question is, what should we do? We can't stay here. We have to do something.*

The platoon leader poked the runner, "Pass the word. Squad leaders and platoon sergeant report to me on the double." The runner, Polowski, slid off into the darkness.

From his vantage point, the lieutenant could see the winking flashes of the enemy rifles and machine guns to the east and along the ridge line to the south. A cynical smile came over the young officer's face as a ludicrous thought crossed his mind. *I wonder what they would say about a situation like this at Fort Benning.*

In a few minutes, the three squad leaders and the platoon sergeant appeared, sliding along the ditch bottom. Second Lieutenant John W. Schneidermann spoke above the racket of surrounding conflict, "We have to make a move. If we stay here, we're dead. We are going to attack straight south up the ridge. We will move out in the same order as we are in now. I'll be right behind the point, man, Ferguson. Sergeant Ridehout will bring up the rear. When we get to within about 50 yards of the enemy trenches, we'll form a skirmish line on my signal. The machine guns will set up and, on my order, open fire on the objective. The guns will fire one box and then cease firing. When I give the word, we will rush the objective."

The non-coms were silent for several seconds, then one asked, "How far is it to the objective?"

The lieutenant answered, "About 450 yards, as near as I can tell."

Silence, then another question, "What will we do when we take the ridge?" The platoon leader replied, "As soon as we reorganize on the objective, we will move east down the ridge and hit the roadblock. One final word, our success will depend on taking the chinks by surprise. I don't think that they expect an attack from this direction. We want to keep down any noise that will give us away."

It was completely dark when the platoon started up the hill. There were fewer men now, some having disappeared on the move from the bridge. The single file of weary soldiers wound slowly up the hill. They maintained an interval of about fifteen feet, as far apart as possible but still able to see the figure ahead. The hill was steep and the going hard, but the little band kept moving. After about twenty-five minutes, the platoon leader signaled a halt. With Sergeant DiAngelo, he moved up to where Ferguson, the point man, was crouched in the snow. The three men scanned the terrain to the front giving special attention to the site of the objective.

Some firing came from the enemy position, but it appeared to be directed at the truck column. The trucks had negotiated the bypass and were now formed on the road but were not moving. The lieutenant had his binoculars out and was carefully sweeping the intended route leading to the crest of the ridge. He silently passed the glasses to the point man who slowly searched the slopes to their front. The infantry soldiers of the platoon remained in position, silent, their thoughts on the coming fight to gain the ridge.

By now, they all knew that the situation was grave. They had seen the convoy stop and could see from their position on the high ground that the Chinese were closing in. They also knew that the wounded men riding in the back of the trucks like so many crippled animals were doomed and that if they were wounded again, they, too, would never leave this desolate valley. Their ties to home, nation, and higher commanders were completely severed. At this moment, the men of the platoon could relate only to the leaders they could see--their squad leader, the platoon sergeant, and their young officer from the Northern Plains.

The point man spoke in a whisper, "Those yellow bastards are not aware of our presence, Lieutenant."

The lieutenant nodded silently. Turning to the squad leader, he asked, "How does it look to you?"

Sergeant DiAngelo nodded silently and replied quietly, "It looks OK to me."

"Let's move out," the platoon leader ordered.

Like a great coiled snake, the platoon moved ahead silently, cautiously, tensions rising. For about fifteen minutes, the single file kept moving. The enemy's position, the objective of their attack, became more distinct. To the north, in the valley and along the road, the battle continued. It was like seeing an epic panorama from the top seats of a giant amphitheater.

As they got closer, it appeared that the number of the enemy was comparatively small. From the sound of their firing, it seemed that only one automatic weapon was there. At a point about seventy yards from the unsuspecting enemy, the platoon leader signaled a halt. He silently directed the men to form a skirmish line. Second Squad to the right, Third Squad to the left, and on a slight wrinkle in the ground between the riflemen, he placed the machine guns. For another ten minutes, the platoon made ready for the attack. Second Lieutenant John W. Schneidermann worked his way along the skirmish line, checking with the squad leaders, and making sure they all knew the game plan.

The platoon leader took a position immediately behind the machine guns along with the platoon sergeant. "Are you ready, Sergeant Cobb?" he quietly asked the machine gun squad leader.

"Yes, Suh," the sergeant confidently responded.

"Open fire," the young officer commanded. Executing a prearranged signal, he raised his right arm and quickly dropped it. Both light .30s came alive with a burst of fire that lighted the area. For about four minutes, the two machine guns chattered like some aggressive metal robots. They were raking the objective with long, ten- and twelve-shot bursts. At the range of seventy yards, the gunners were able to concentrate on their targets with maximum effect. John Schneidermann closely watched the guns, and as he saw them stop firing and raise the covers, he gave the order to cease firing. Immediately he leaped to his feet and shouted a command, "Let's go! Let's hit 'em!"

The men in the two rifle squads jumped to a standing position, and with their weapons in a firing position, they headed for the objective. All the reverses and discouragements, all the fears and heartbreaks were forgotten. Only one overwhelming goal was in their minds--close on the enemy and kill them all. The men moved forward at a rapid walk, firing at any suspected target. They closed the distance in a few short minutes. At the objective, no living enemy remained. It appeared that the machine gun fire had caught the Chinese riflemen unaware. Those surviving the concentrated hail of machine gun fire had apparently fled down the slope to the south.

The riflemen swarmed over the objective with the wild enthusiasm of a football receiver crossing the goal line. The platoon leader had led the charge and had closed on the enemy position along with the skirmish line. Despite the biting cold, the fatigue, and the fear, the infantrymen were in a state of high exhilaration. "We did it! We did it! I didn't think we could, but we did it!"

Winning in the combat infantry is a tonic, and they had indeed won the fight. They had launched an attack from an untenable position, marched across mountainous terrain, and assaulted an entrenched enemy. They had beaten the Chinese at their own game, man-to-man infantry fighting.

Second Lieutenant John W. Schneidermann sat on the edge of the trench taking stock of the situation. Images of the fight were still etched in his mind: the dark figures of the advancing soldiers, firing as they stepped along; the crumpled bodies of the defenders; the cheers and shouts; the brown earth and logs of the entrenchments. Now the thoughts of the present passed through his mind: *What a great fight! We won against all odds! What incredibly good fortune. We're going to win this thing after all, but what to do now? The mission--what is the mission?*

The platoon runner, Polowski, approached from the darkness, "Are you OK, Sir?"

"Yeah, I'm fine, Polowski. Thanks. Go back down to the machine guns and have Sergeant Cobb move them up here."

"Yes, Sir." The runner slipped away through the pale light.

After the capture of an objective, there is invariably a period of confusion for the attackers. During this time, they are vulnerable to a counterattack. Modern infantry doctrine dictates that the defense of the newly won position is critical. In that light, the platoon leader ordered the riflemen to form a hasty perimeter defense.

The fortifications along the ridge now occupied by the platoon had been originally built by the 5th Marines. Most were facing to the north, but there were a few bunkers on the south side of the ridge. Sergeant Cobb and his machine gun squad arrived on the site and were placed on the perimeter facing west toward the higher ground. The lieutenant spoke to Sergeant Ridehout, the platoon sergeant, "Round up the squad leaders right away. We'll meet at this bunker."

"Yes, Sir," the sergeant replied as, minutes later, the non-coms came shuffling out of the darkness.

The platoon leader spoke in a low voice, "You did a fantastic job, men. You executed the attack flawlessly. Nobody could have done better. We made a night movement across unknown terrain and knocked out a dug-in enemy, all without any losses. Now we have to keep going. We can't stay here. We'll move down the ridge line to the east and hit that roadblock. It's about 500 yards away and all downhill. We'll use the same formation we used coming up here. 2nd Squad in the lead. We'll maintain silence. If we run into any opposition, we'll return fire and take them out." The platoon leader continued, "How is the ammunition supply?"

The machine gun squad leader spoke up, "We have two boxes for each gun, Suh." The rifle squad leaders, DiAngelo and 0'Mally, reported about 100 rounds per rifle and about 200 rounds per AR. I'll be right behind the point," the lieutenant announced. "We'll move out in twenty minutes. Are there any questions?"

The four non-coms sat silently staring at the ground.... Finally, one of the squad leaders, DiAngelo, spoke up, "Are we going to make it out of here, Lieutenant?"

A feeling of isolation and despair suddenly settled over the little group. It was now Thursday, and the men of the task force had been fighting since Monday night when the forces of the People's Liberation Army had suddenly poured out of the frigid mountains. They were physically exhausted from the constant exertion and the unrelenting cold. They had seen their comrades struck down and knew that they could easily be next. They knew that the task force was breaking up and that there was no help coming to rescue them or to provide any support. A sense of self-preservation was building in the minds of the beleaguered men.

The young officer stood up and slowly looked at each man. He began to speak in a firm, steady voice, "Well, Sergeant, I sure hope we make it. I know one thing for sure. We have to keep trying. If we can make it down the ridge to the roadblock and put it out of action, it could mean life or death to the truck convoy." The lieutenant continued, "Thanks to your abilities as leaders and as soldiers, we are hanging together, and we are winning. Now we must keep moving and keep fighting. Now get back to the squads and be ready to roll."

The men got up slowly and, with some effort, started walking back to their battered squads. The lieutenant turned to the platoon sergeant and asked, "You don't know what happened to Garza?"

The sergeant replied, "The last time I saw him was down on the road."

The lieutenant looked at the quiet soldier and inquired, "How are you doing, Sergeant?"

"I'm OK for now."

After twenty minutes, the platoon began forming in their march formation in preparation for the move down the ridge line. They started along a faint trail maintaining an interval of 5 to 6 yards. They moved slowly and deliberately, ready for instant action. They felt as though they were at the top of the world with a spectacular view of the valleys to the north and the south. The sights and sounds of the battle were still coming from the land below. A sense of isolation was still gripping the tired soldiers as they kept up their steady pace. As they moved silently down the spine of the ridge, a picture of the colonial rangers came to mind—green-and leather-clad fighters with their muskets and bayonets on their audacious mission against heavy odds.

The hill was covered with scrub trees and patches of sparse brush hindering the soldiers as they stepped along the dim trail. No one challenged the silent infantrymen as they kept moving closer and ever closer to their objective, the bend in the road. The men were moving as if in a stupor. The long hours of combat, the cold weather, and the realization that the task force was facing destruction were taking their toll. The men moved now because there was nothing else to do. As the platoon closed the distance to the roadblock, the battle sounds grew louder. The soldiers kept their steady, easterly pace toward the objective. About one hundred yards out, the platoon leader moved up to the point man and signaled a halt. The men dropped to the ground and remained motionless. The lieutenant turned to the squad leader, who had come up from the rear, "Sergeant, I am going down to the road. I think that the block might have already been secured. Wait here."

With the runner close behind, the platoon leader moved cautiously forward. As he neared the road, he heard voices coming from the area of the roadblock. The two men edged to within a few yards of the position and listened intently. The sound of familiar words filtered back to the men in the underbrush. The lieutenant turned to the runner and whispered, "I believe that the roadblock has already been captured. Let's go down and check it out."

The two men cautiously made their way to the road where a group of U.S. soldiers was congregated around the roadblock. Second Lieutenant John W. Schneidermann walked up to the group and inquired, "Who is in command here?"

A stocky captain limping along on a makeshift cane answered, "I guess I am." Second Lieutenant John W. Schneidermann identified himself and described the disposition of his platoon. The captain spoke in a halting voice, "I don't have to tell you that the situation around here is total chaos. The command structure has fallen apart. We are trying to get the truck convoy moving.

Nobody wants to follow orders. I don't know what's going to happen." He paused momentarily and then continued, "I would say that you should move down the road to the south. If there are any enemy roadblocks, see if you can take them out."

The lieutenant replied, "I'll give it a try, Sir, and if my company comes through, would you tell the CO where I went?"

The captain nodded, "I'll do that, Lieutenant, and good luck."

The scene around the roadblock was one of disorganization and confusion. The sounds of men crunching along the gravel road and calling back and forth were audible for some distance.

The platoon leader gave a silent prayer of thanks that he and the platoon didn't have to assault the roadblock. "Polowski, go back and bring up the men, and I'll wait here," he ordered.

Yes, Sir," the runner replied as he headed back up the ridge.

After a few minutes, the point man, Ferguson, emerged from the brush, followed by Sergeant DiAngelo. The platoon leader signaled the point man to keep moving down the road to the south.

The platoon filed past, shuffling along, heads down, calling on their last reserves of energy. The lieutenant joined the column as it went by, falling in right behind the lead squad. It was a grim scene along the narrow dirt road: the darkness, the sporadic firing, the desolate landscape. The men trudged on, their movements almost automated. After several minutes, the platoon leader moved forward and located the 2nd Squad leader. "Call a halt, Sergeant," he ordered.

At the signal, the men stopped, dropped to the ground, and sat motionless. The lieutenant quietly spoke to his squad leader, "Our mission is to keep moving south and clear the road of any blocks. How are your men making it?" the platoon leader inquired.

"Well, they are still moving," the sergeant responded.

"Good. Keep plugging." The lieutenant moved back along the file of silent infantrymen to the rear of the platoon. The platoon sergeant and the two squad leaders were together at the tail of the column. The lieutenant repeated his order and asked the non-coms, "How is everyone doing back here?"

"Everyone is pretty well beat, but they're still moving."

The thoughts of the men were currently focused on the basic elements--sleep, warmth, food, safety. All other hopes and desires had faded away. This has been true of the combat soldier since the dawn of time. The trappings of society were not pertinent anymore. The spark of self-respect and loyalty to your comrades was the final driving force. Second Lieutenant John Schneidermann walked forward along the right edge of the roadway toward the head of the platoon column. The riflemen and gunners sat beside the grade. There was none of the usual, casual conversation, no light talk or horseplay, only silent stares. As the platoon leader followed along the line, his eyes scanned each individual. The young soldiers were looking at the ground or off into the distance. These were the men who had survived. They had fought the tough peasant soldiers of China and had come through. They were now waiting, resting before the next ordeal they knew was coming. Their clothes were shiny with grease, dirty, torn, and rumpled. They could have been the modern version of the light infantry of the Army of the Valley. They were battered but still held their weapons, and they still presented a certain air of competence.

Only fifteen men remained: four in the 2nd Squad, which was in the lead; four in the 3rd Squad, which was bringing up the rear; four in the machine guns; the platoon leader and runner who were right behind the lead squad; and the platoon sergeant who was the last man in the file.

It was about six road miles to the forward Marine positions. If the way was reasonably clear and with a little luck, they could still make it. The men of the platoon stood up on the signal of the young officer and again started down the narrow dirt track. The column kept moving with a steady shuffling gait.

A ghostly column of burned-out vehicles and a disabled tank loomed out of the darkness, a reminder of the destructive power of the Chinese infantry. These were part of the 31st Medical Company that had been ambushed on the first night of the enemy attack. The tank was from the 31st Infantry Tank Company. It was lost in an attempt to take Hill 1221 from the south. The platoon marched by the empty hulks in silence. The point man, PFC Andrew J. Ferguson, set the pace for the file. As he methodically stepped forward, he searched the terrain ahead and to the left, and to the right. Occasionally the point man would signal a halt with an upraised right arm. The men following would drop down and bring their weapons to the ready. Always a possibility the object of the point man's suspicion could erupt in a burst of enemy fire. The point man moved carefully forward, checking the menacing position. When the area was deemed clear, he would return to the line of march and wave a "forward" with a downward sweep of his right arm. Battle sounds continued to the north and east. The moon began to rise, casting a pale light on the landscape. The men of the platoon were alone again, isolated on the battlefield, the figure to their front and back their only human contact.

About a road mile south of the saddle, the dirt track made another sharp bend. As the undersized platoon, hardly more than a squad, rounded the turn, the point man signaled a halt. The men stopped and stood motionless on the right shoulder of the grade. Something had awakened the point man's sense of danger. He stood stock still, looking, listening. The moonlight shone on the frozen landscape, outlining rocks, trees, and depressions in the ground. The point man, Ferguson, motioned the men in the column down with a movement of his right arm. The rattle of distant firing came across the cold night air, and a light wind swept the area. The point man stepped out toward a pile of rubble about fifty yards ahead and east of the road. In an instant, frozen in time, an automatic weapon began firing from the suspicious pile of rubble, the bullets sweeping the road.

The blast caught the infantrymen in the process of dropping to a firing position. Those who had already reached the safety of the ditch were protected from the searing stream of bullets as they passed over the road. With speed driven by instinct and fear, the men of the rifle platoon brought their weapons to bear and began firing. The two machine guns took a few more seconds to go into action but were soon both firing. The combined clamor of all the firing created a deafening roar. The two light .30s were within a few yards of each other, pouring a hail of bullets toward flashes of the enemy gun. The rifles added their deadly effect to the effort. As quickly as it started, the firing tapered off to a few ragged shots.

The point man who had dropped where he stood cautiously rose and started for the enemy position. In a few anxious seconds, he scrambled to the base of the hostile emplacement. The point man, with a quick motion, snatched a fragmentation grenade from his web suspenders, jerked out the pin, and tossed it into the enemy position. The deadly device exploded with a loud blast. Silence. The point man quickly repeated the process, and another grenade landed at the source of the enemy firing. All quiet. The point man vaulted over the rocks and into the heart of the gun position. No movement or sound. The point man called back to the column, "They're all dead. Hold your fire."

PFC Andrew Ferguson walked slowly back to the road. The infantry soldiers of the platoon slowly stood and looked around, wondering about their losses. In the lead squad, three men were lying dead in the ditch. They had caught the initial blast of the machine gun fire, which had miraculously missed the point man altogether. The men with the machine gun had landed in the ditch just before the bullets swept over the road, escaping injury completely except for the last man who was wounded. The first two men in the last squad, the squad leader, and the point, had delayed too long and were fatally hit.

Lieutenant Schneidermann was standing on the right shoulder of the road just behind the lead squad. He dropped to the protection of the ditch just a split second too late. As he was slipping to the ground, a jolt hit his left leg like a blow from a club. A jacketed bullet had passed through his leg about six inches above the knee but had not touched the bone. At the same time, a second bullet hit his left shoulder. This one was not a direct hit but a ricochet that was probably tumbling when it struck. The platoon sergeant crawled forward to the portion of the ditch where the platoon leader was lying motionless, face down. The runner, Polowski, worked on the still form. Finally, the lieutenant rose to a partial sitting position. The shock of the bullets had left him dazed, but he was still conscious. He felt no particular sensation of pain.

Polowski spoke up in a voice filled with despair. "It looks like our luck ran out, Sir."

The young officer turned to the platoon sergeant and asked, "How many got hit?"

The platoon sergeant answered in a shaken voice, " At least four KIA and two WIA."

Farther down the road to the south, a second enemy machine gun began firing. The range was so great that the effect on the platoon was minimal. Now thoughts were passing through the young lieutenant's head like a whirlwind: *I wonder how bad I'm hit... there really isn't much pain... what a disaster... what are we going to do? We can't stay here."*

The position of the platoon was precarious. From all indications, the enemy held the road to the south in force. Some scattered shots were coming from the hill mass to the north, which signaled the presence of an enemy of unknown strength. The truck column, along with the remainder of the task force, was fighting for their very existence and could offer no aid. In the space of seconds, disaster had struck the already beleaguered platoon.

Lieutenant John Schneidermann tried to sit up and then stand. By testing the injured leg, he found he could walk with some effort. The machine gun squad leader appeared, crawling to where the small command group was gathered. The platoon leader inquired, "How is your situation, Sergeant Cobb?"

"One man hit, Suh. He ain't too good, but we'll try to carry him along."

The point man, Ferguson, came ducking from the south, stooping low. "I think there are more chinks to the south, Lieutenant. I went down the road about fifty yards, and I could hear them talking. There are only two of us left in the lead squad," the point man reported in a serious voice.

All the enemy fire had ended. The moon had risen higher, brightening the area, and showing outlines of scattered trees, rocks, and the still forms of the men lying on the road. A light wind drifted across the scene. The ever-present cold continued probing into the layers of clothing, grasping at the very souls of the forlorn group of soldiers. The platoon leader spoke in a low steady voice, "We can't keep going down the road. We'll have to make it to the reservoir and then head south on the ice. We'll keep going south until we get to the Marine lines. Take all the ammunition and destroy the extra weapons. We better move out as soon as possible because the chinks will be coming here to see what happened."

Sergeant Cobb spoke up in a slow, soft drawl, "Shall we take one gun, Suh? We still have a box and a half of ammo."

The lieutenant answered, "That's OK. Take one gun." The point man and the other rifleman cautiously crawled to the road and quickly took the weapons and ammunition from the inert bodies. "OK, men, let's move out. Ferguson, take the lead," the platoon leader called.

In a few minutes, the battered remnant of the platoon started toward the shore of the lake about a half mile distant. A total of ten men were left in the ragged file: the point man was in the lead, followed by a rifleman, the platoon leader, the runner, the three men of the machine gun squad, an AR man, a rifleman, and the platoon sergeant. The last two men were helping the wounded machine gunner, one on each side supporting him. He had thrown an arm over the shoulder of the two able-bodied men. The group climbed over the railroad grade and headed directly for the reservoir. The lieutenant had given his rifle to Sergeant Cobb and, with the aid of a makeshift crutch, was making credible progress.

The gravity of the situation was dawning on the platoon leader. In spite of his wounds, John Schneidermann was at least thinking clearly. *How could this have happened...? In the space of a minute everything fell apart.... What an incredible stroke of bad luck.... That one chink position, I should have been more careful... Maybe I was overconfident.... We have to keep going.... With a little luck, we can still make it.*

The ragged remnant of the platoon kept moving at a slow but steady pace. The two wounded men were still moving but at a reduced speed. At a point about halfway to the shoreline, the platoon leader signaled a halt. The men sank to the rough, snow-covered ground for a much-needed break.

They sat there in a kind of stupor, breathing in short, heavy breaths. The moon was still out, visible, casting a pale light over the rough landscape.

As the men of the platoon sat in a ragged line, a group of dark figures appeared to the north. They were moving directly toward the platoon in a compact formation. The platoon leader turned to the machine gun squad leader, "Set up your gun, Sergeant."

"Yes, Suh."·

The figures became more distinct. There were about twelve, no, more like twenty. The point man crawled back to the platoon leader and asked, "Who are those guys, Lieutenant?"

The lieutenant tersely replied, "I don't know. Pass the word to prepare to fire on my order."

The point man, Ferguson, slid back along the platoon line. The figures moved closer. Through his field glasses, the platoon leader could make out the flapping, dog-ear caps, and padded uniforms. The men were coming at a trot. The men of the platoon lay transfixed, their eyes glued to the oncoming soldiers. The enemy group was now within two hundred yards and closing fast. Short of a hundred yards, the enemy unit abruptly stopped. Talking could be heard drifting across the snow.

Second Lieutenant John W. Schneidermann firmly gave the order, "Open fire, Sergeant Cobb."

The machine gun leaped into action and was instantly joined by the rifles. The initial volley fell on the standing group of Chinese infantrymen. Some could be seen down, and the rest were running back toward the hill. The men of the platoon, driven by frustration and anger, kept up a steady fire on the fleeing enemy. The weapons of the U.S. soldiers finally quit firing. Silence.

The platoon sergeant approached from the rear of the file. He reported in a solemn voice, "Smitty didn't make it, Sir."

The two men stared at the ground in silence. Sergeant Cobb, the machine gun leader, finally spoke up, "That's the last of the machine gun ammo, Suh."

"Break up the gun, Sergeant Cobb. It's no good to us now," the lieutenant ordered.

"I sure hate to do that, Suh, but I agree," the squad leader answered.

The men slowly got to their feet. Sergeant Cobb, in a few quick motions, disassembled the machine gun and threw the parts in different directions. He grabbed the gun by the barrel and slammed it against the frozen ground. With the reservoir less than five hundred yards away, the little command pressed on.

The beleaguered group finally came to the edge of the reservoir and walked out on the ice with only nine men left now, in deplorable condition. "Is the ice strong enough to walk on?" someone called out.

The young lieutenant from the Northern Plains, who had walked on the frozen lakes of Minnesota, replied, "Don't worry about the ice. It will hold wild horses."

The men were in a state of exhaustion, both physically and mentally. Every movement was an effort. The young officer could feel fatigue setting in. There was a growing urge to stop and rest, but to stop and rest invited death by freezing. Tracks in the snow that covered the ice indicated that a previous body of soldiers had gone that way. The moon continued to cast its pale light over the flat surface of the snow-covered lake.

"How far will we have to walk, Sir?" asked the runner.

"About three or four miles," replied the lieutenant. The party kept moving, stopping briefly every few minutes to rest. John Schneidermann's wounds began to ache. The shock was beginning to wear off. The loss of blood, the cold, and the fatigue were taking their toll on his mind and body. His blood-soaked jacket and field pants had frozen, and the wounds had clotted over. The left shoulder wound was particularly painful as each step jolted the injury. The leg wound was swelling, filling out the trouser leg.

A sense of isolation descended on the forlorn little party as they made their way slowly across the ice toward the U.S.-held town at the south end of the frozen reservoir. To the east, in the vicinity of Hill 1221, signs of battle were still visible. Sounds of firing carried across the open ice, and flashes of weapons were clearly visible. All semblance of unit cohesion was fading. Escape and survival were uppermost in the minds of the beleaguered men. They had been beaten by the peasant soldiers in their nondescript, padded uniforms. The relentless onslaught of the Chinese infantry and the never-ceasing cold had smashed the fighting capabilities of the mechanized U.S. soldiers. Now if they could just get away, away from the blood, from the gunfire, from the biting cold.

They plodded on with no appearance of any formation. John Schneidermann was getting weaker, his resolve failing. But he was still responsible, still in command, still leading his platoon though only a few were left. This drove him on, one step, another step, keep moving. To stop now for any length of time would be a disaster. Thoughts kept flowing through his mind: *They hadn't really won... The shadow figures kept coming despite the best of efforts... If only we could have some support... The platoon is still going to survive if only we can keep going.* His left leg was beginning to stiffen, moving as if it were wooden.

Across the ice near the edge of the lake, a group of dark figures was seen heading out on the reservoir toward them. The runner, Polowski, spoke up in a hoarse voice, "Lieutenant, the chinks are coming after us."

Mesmerized, the men turned and stared at the five dark figures that were moving on the ice. Second Lieutenant John W. Schneidermann was now facing the end of the line. If the pathetic remnants of his platoon were overtaken by the pursuing enemy, they would all be killed or captured.

"What have we got for ammo?" the platoon leader asked in a tense voice. The total supply of ammunition amounted to three clips of rifle cartridges, about 24 shots. The BAR had been thrown away, its ammunition gone. Seven serviceable rifles remained in the group.

The platoon leader gave a terse order, "Sergeant Rideout, take the men and move out. I just can't keep up. I'll hold them off. Give me my rifle and the clips, and get going."

No one spoke or moved. The figures of the Chinese soldiers became large as they rapidly came closer. "Get moving, you men!" The lieutenant was still in command, the blood of the ancient warriors of the north country coming to the surface. John Schneidermann could hear himself shouting at the top of his voice, "I said move out, now!"

The moonlight filtered over the snow-covered ice, an unreal scene. Here were the survivors of the proud and carefree U.S. Army caught like wild animals, like the jackrabbits surrounded by hunters on the snow-covered northern plains.

Finally, Sergeant Cobb spoke up in his smooth, quiet drawl, "We ain't goin' to leave you, Suh." No one spoke.

"Let's get going then," the lieutenant answered wearily. With that, the men started in a shuffling run, heading toward the southern end of the reservoir. Sergeant Cobb took the lieutenant by the right arm, threw it around his neck, and took off at a slow run.

The men, in a renewed burst of energy, made some initial progress across the snow-covered ice. Because of their better physical condition, the men led by the platoon sergeant began gaining ground. The lieutenant, assisted by the machine gun leader, valiantly kept up a steady pace. For ten minutes, the grim race continued. The lead group of U.S. soldiers was making good progress, the two men in the rear were falling back, and the pursuing enemy infantrymen were gaining.

For some unknown reason, the Chinese riflemen stopped, raised their weapons, and fired several shots. Lieutenant John Schneidermann and the machine gun leader kept up their shuffling run. Slowly, the squad leader seemed to relax, stop, and then fall to the surface of the reservoir, knocking the young officer down in the process. The Chinese soldiers stared at the two fallen men, who were about 250 yards distant. After standing in their position for about a minute, all but one of the peasant fighters turned and began walking back toward the shoreline. The single rifleman continued toward the two fallen U.S. soldiers. A rifle bullet had hit Sergeant Thomas R.R. Cobb, U.S. Army, RA 179654, age 20, in the small of the back. He fell in a heap on top of the rifle he was carrying in his right hand. He made no sound as he fell, his eyes closed, and his heart stopped.

To the lead group, who were now far out on the frozen surface, it appeared that both men had been hit by the volley of rifle fire. They kept up their pace heading for the south end. Second Lieutenant John W. Schneidermann was not hit and landed partially on top of the fallen sergeant. Sharp pain shot from his two wounds. He thought: *At least they're not frozen solid.*

The lieutenant made a half roll to a partial sitting position and stayed there, trying to regain his breath. His breath was coming in short puffs, visible in the frigid air. Scenes from the past flashed through his consciousness: the black soil as it rolled from the plow, the sunset over the flat prairie, the girl in the blue checkered dress, the reservoir, the village of Hagaru-ri, the Marines, warmth, safety, food.

The single Chinese rifleman slowly walked toward the two fallen men. A sense of curiosity pushed him on in the direction of the dark figures on the ice.

Usually, most Americans had something of value--gloves, rations, things that were vital to the men who survived by utilizing captured supplies. The padded soldier was a member of the Peoples Liberation Army's 80th Division, the unit that had been attacking the U.S. Army troops for the past four nights. They had essentially destroyed the 31st RCT despite the black war birds that were constantly attacking during the daylight hours with their firebombs and rockets. The fearsome tracked vehicles with their rapid-firing guns were now silent hulks, their guns quiet and their engines cold. The battle had gone as their leaders had predicted. The 80th Division had been hit hard, but victory was now within its grasp.

Lieutenant John Schneidermann lay still, trying to clear his mind. He knew that this was a desperate situation. Sergeant Cobb was dead, no doubt about it. No response, no movement. His left arm was almost useless and hung limp at his side. The rifle was hopelessly caught under the fallen squad leader. The platoon leader's strength was failing. He looked across the ice at the approaching enemy rifleman. At this point, the Chinese soldier was close enough to distinctly see the two fallen Americans. They both looked dead but perhaps not. He moved his rifle to a ready position.

The Asian soldier was young, short, and stocky. He came from a rural part of China where his entire family, including two grandparents, lived on ten acres of land. He had been a soldier in the People's Liberation Army for three years. He was tough, hardy, and self-reliant. He had listened to the political officers as they extolled the glories of the Peoples' Republic. The enemy rifleman stopped about twenty-five feet from the two fallen Americans. He carefully viewed the two still forms with a searching gaze. One man was definitely dead. A pool of blood was spreading onto the ice creating a steaming red circle. The Chinese soldier had seen death in many forms in his twenty years, so it made little impression on him. These well-equipped, well-fed Americans could also die. Their equipment and unlimited supplies did not protect them.

The other man was still also, and his eyes were closed, but was he dead? The young peasant soldier of China looked carefully at his fallen enemy and then walked up to within fifteen feet. He held his Mauser rifle at a low port with his left hand.

Second Lieutenant John W. Schneidermann momentarily felt a surge of unexpected energy. He opened his eyes and stared into the impassive face of the enemy standing in front of him. The platoon leader, in a sudden motion, rolled to a sitting position. The Chinese rifleman gazed steadily into the face of the man sitting in the snow. He was obviously hurt from the looks of the bloodstained jacket and field pants. No weapon was visible. Not a threat. What to do? The pale blue eyes that were locked in his gaze did not seem to show fear. The oriental soldier had seen fear, too, like that in the eyes of a condemned man about to be executed. There was no trace of the frantic, wild stare that spoke of uncontrolled fear. No hurry. It could be that the American will die at any time. He won't survive anyway. Maybe it would be doing him a favor to shoot him. For a few fleeting seconds, the eyes of Ancient China, a centuries-old civilization, a civilization of silk, of literature, of art, looked into the eyes of Northern Europe, a newer civilization, a civilization of steel, of law, and of commerce. The two representatives of their own different worlds, for a brief space of time, seemed drawn to each other. They were drawn out of curiosity, then out of comradery, then out of brotherhood. Their looks both seemed to say: "Why are we here trying to harm each other?" If there was a common language, perhaps they could discuss things they both knew about: land, crops, family…. The moon cast its pale light, and the cold wind lightly blew across the frozen snow. The two soldiers were alone, alone in their own private worlds.

Reluctantly, the brief meeting came to an end. With a quick motion, the peasant soldier worked the bolt of his venerable Mauser to the open position with his right hand. Balancing the rifle in his left hand, he reached for a full, five-shot clip in his cartridge belt.

Second Lieutenant John W. Schneidermann, in an instantaneous movement, reached under his field jacket for his .45 automatic pistol. The weapon was resting in the shoulder holster, loaded with six shots in the magazine and one shot in the chamber. With two fingers, he flipped open the leather strap holding in the weapon. His hand closed around the handle of the pistol. With a swift, continuous pull, the grey steel weapon slid from under the field jacket. A look of alarm came over the face of the Chinese soldier. He had made a serious mistake. Frantically, he groped for a loaded clip. The hammer of the .45 was in the forward "half cock" position. The young officer from the Northern Plains, with a deft motion of his right thumb, cocked the weapon. The pistol came up to the firing position in what seemed like slow motion. Experience took over, all movement was automatic now. Find the target in the sights, steady, and squeeze the trigger. The .45 roared, and a flash of fire lighted up the night; the pistol flashed again and again. The first bullet struck the Chinese soldier squarely in the chest, the second hit his right shoulder, and the third missed entirely. The padded infantryman pitched to one side and fell to the ice, his old rifle landing with a clatter.

Except for the low moaning of the wind, a silence fell over the reservoir. For what seemed like an imponderable length of time, John Schneidermann sat where he was, his right hand holding the pistol, his breathing heavy. Now was the time for action if there was to be survival. Slowly, with pain racking his injured leg and shoulder, the young soldier rose to his feet. He stood for several moments, shaking, looking around. The two still forms lay sprawled where they had fallen. The lieutenant let down the hammer of the pistol and shoved it back into the holster. Wobbling, he started after the remainder of the platoon. One step, then another, trying to stifle the pain and keep moving.

After what seemed like an interminable length of time, the platoon leader approached a point halfway to the Marine line. The landscape had changed, with the battle area slowly fading in the distance. The going was difficult. The wounds were throbbing with pain at every step, but the young officer kept on. The hills on the west side of the reservoir began to appear more distinctly. No one else was in sight, but tracks in the snow told of people who had passed earlier. Actually, it was a most attractive and picturesque view: the hills, the snow-covered ice, and the moon overhead. The lieutenant had kept his pistol and binoculars, but everything else was gone: his rifle, map case, and sleeping bag.

In the distance to the south, across the level ice, a file of dark figures appeared. Second Lieutenant John W. Schneidermann stopped and looked carefully. He thought: *They've got to be friendly. No enemy would be coming from that direction."* He slowly started walking forward. The figures kept getting closer and closer. The lieutenant stopped again, studying the oncoming squad. *Those are U.S. helmets. They have to be Americans.* Finally, into closer view came a squad of eight men who could be identified by their camouflaged helmets as U.S. Marines. The squad stopped, and the leader, the second in line, walked up to the platoon leader. The Marine was a young giant, 6' 6" tall and muscular.

"Are you Lieutenant Schneidermann?" he asked.

"That right," John Schneidermann replied.

"Good. Your platoon sergeant made us go looking for you. He said he would kick the crap out of me if I didn't," the Marine non-com stated with a grin. "I believe he really meant it."

The Marine squad had brought along a litter which they unfolded. The giant non-com picked up the battered infantry soldier and gently placed him on the stretcher. With a husky Marine on each corner of the litter, the squad headed for the south end of the reservoir at a fast clip.

"Your boys made it to our outpost," the Marine squad leader commented, "We sent them on to the aid station."

"Glad to hear that. Thanks for picking me up. I don't know if I could have made it," the platoon leader said in a weak voice.

"Our pleasure, Lieutenant. We are always eager to help you Army guys," the Marine said with a laugh.

The time it took to cover the distance to the Marine lines seemed to go by in a flash. With the moon overhead and the squad of Marines carrying him along, the young infantry officer started to relax.

The blur of the aid station passed by in a haze of faces of the navy corpsmen, doctors, orderlies, the other casualties; the medicinal odor of anesthetics, the heat from the stoves, of alcohol; the sounds of tearing cloth, of low voices, of moans; the comfort of clean bandages, plasma, a cot, warmth, hot soup.

"That .45 is my personal property, Doc. I expect to have it when I leave here."

"Don't worry, Lieutenant. I'll see that you get it."

The medical team worked over the wounded officer with skill and haste. They cleaned the wounds, extracted a bullet from the shoulder joint, and applied bandages. A series of antibiotics was injected, and plasma was administered. Second Lieutenant John W. Schneidermann floated off into a drug-induced sleep.

The characters of the past few days and nights passed through his troubled mind in a distorted vision. The men of the platoon were marching by in a single file, silent, with passive facial expressions. They were in a dusty column, clad in faded green, summer uniforms and worn, shiny helmets. There was Sergeant Pratt, the squad leaders, the riflemen, the gunners, Sergeant Cobb, and the faces of the ROK soldiers, strange in a wild, frightening way. They marched by with a nod, a slight wave, a signal to join them. They moved out of sight as they progressed toward the other side of a deep chasm.

Following the Americans were other faceless figures in their quilted uniforms and caps with earflaps. They all looked serene, calm, and complacent. At last, lagging, was a lone Chinese soldier. As his face, plain, calm, impassive, came into view, it was the face of the lone enemy rifleman on the ice. He turned and looked at the platoon leader in a calm manner with no hostility showing, no look of condemnation. He seemed to say, "You won. That is the way of things. I hold no grudge."

A jolting motion woke up Lieutenant John Schneidermann. His stretcher was being loaded into a Marine ambulance for a short ride to the crude airstrip. After what seemed to be a long wait, the wounded from several ambulances were loaded on a C-47 transport. The engines roared, and the plane shook and vibrated as it bounced down the rough runway and finally leaped into the air for a brief flight to another world.

# Home

As the massive Ford truck continued down the gravel road, the driver flipped a switch on the dash. A bank of lights went on, giving the truck the appearance of a rolling, illuminated sign with lamps of amber, red, and white. The driver shifted up through several gears, gradually picking up speed. At forty-five miles per hour the truck held at a steady velocity, moving smoothly along the level road. The snow began to increase in volume, coming down in large wet flakes that drifted, covering the landscape and everything on it. After about three miles, the gravel road came to an intersection with an asphalt highway. The truck slowed for the stop sign getting down to a speed of ten miles per hour. The driver turned on his signal lights and crept through the intersection, executing a left turn. On the blacktop highway, the truck again increased its speed up to forty-five miles per hour. A small village consisting of a filling station, a few scattered houses, and a small elevator appeared through the snow. After crossing a double-tracked railroad, the truck pulled up to a stop sign at a state highway. The driver slowed to a complete stop, shifted into the lowest gear, let out the clutch, and slowly pulled onto the highway with a right turn. After driving down the highway for about six city blocks, the truck turned into an area about an acre in size lying between the highway and the railroad. Sitting in the area was a grain-handling complex consisting of several large, circular steel bins, an elevator leg, a dump pit, some smaller overhead hopper bins, and a grain drier. The truck rolled in to the complex and pulled to a halt on the dump platform. The back of the truck box was directly over the grated pit opening. John Schneidermann opened the cab door and climbed to the ground. The drier was running with the burner roaring and clouds of steam rising upward. A figure clad in jeans, a hooded sweatshirt, and rubber overshoes stepped out from behind the drier. "Can you take another load, Jim?" the driver asked.

"No problem, John. Go ahead and dump it," Jim replied.

John Schneidermann walked to the truck and climbed into the cab. With a practiced hand, he engaged the power take-off and opened the hydraulic valve to the hoist cylinders. The massive steel box filled with six hundred bushels of newly harvested, shelled corn began to rise.

As the front of the box rose, Jim called out, "Hold it." The driver shut off the truck engine. Jim opened the gate at the lower end of the back section of the box, and a cascade of bright yellow corn poured out and down into the pit. Jim had started the elevator leg which gently hoisted the corn upward at the rate of fifty bushels per minute.

John Schneidermann climbed out of the truck and walked back to where the corn was streaming out. "How are things going, Jim?" the farmer asked.

"Pretty good. The propane is getting a little low, but I called Art," Jim replied.

"Yeah, he is supposed to keep the tank full, but I suppose he's running behind. We should be OK," John Schneidermann commented. The avalanche of corn continued to flow from the truck box like a golden arc.

"How much longer can the combines keep going?" Jim mused.

"I think they're about done. I better give Bill a call," John said as he walked around to the truck cab and climbed in. He grabbed the radio mike from the dash and pressed the key,

"Bill, are you on?"

"Go ahead."

"How's it going out there?" Bill asked.

"We are about out of business," John replied.

"OK, why don't you come in with the truck and we'll wrap it up."

"OK."

Jim called, "Raise it up." The truck engine started, and the box moved up with no sound or vibration. "Hold it," Jim shouted.

John Schneidermann dismounted from the truck and walked back to where Jim was standing. The two men silently watched the corn pour out, mesmerized by the golden stream. John finally spoke, "How long did you want to work tonight, Jim?"

"I thought I would stay around till maybe 7:30. I'll unload the last truck and then shut her down," Jim answered.

"Sounds good. If this snow keeps up, we'll probably be out of action in the field for a while," the farmer commented. "We'll see what it looks like tomorrow."

"OK, John."

The snow continued to drift down almost vertically. With the fading of daylight, the two mercury-vapor yard lights came on, illuminating the work area where the unloading was taking place. The men stood silently, the snow piling up on their sweatshirts. John Schneidermann broke the silence, "I suppose we better start thinking about getting some equipment into the shop."

"I guess we should," Jim answered.

"What should we tackle first?" John queried.

"I was thinking about the old planter," Jim replied thoughtfully.

"Probably as good as any," the older man responded. Silence.

The flow of the yellow grain was slowing, the big stream finally splitting into two parts. Jim reached for a hoe-like tool and began cleaning out the corners of the truck box. John Schneidermann walked to the front of the truck, reached into the cab, and worked the hydraulic valve lever. The massive steel box, freed of its load, began a gentle descent.

Off on one side of the driveway stood a small wood building. The two men walked to the door of the building and went in. Inside the small, brightly lighted structure were the electric switches and starters that controlled the many motors that powered the complex system. The building, about ten by twelve feet in size, also contained a built-in desk, a counter, a small refrigerator, and a coffee pot on an electric hot plate. Several well-worn chairs rounded out the furnishings. Three wide, automotive-type windows provided a clear view of the operating part of the grain system. The two men each poured a cup of coffee and dropped into a chair. Both sat in silence, sipping their coffee and soaking up the warmth of the building. The noise of the drier was muted by the insulated walls of the control structure. Steam continued to rise from the drier in great, white, irregular clouds. The light from the mercury vapor lamps cast a pattern of shadows formed by the structural steel of the complex. The older man broke the silence as he spoke quietly. "Well, Jim, another season coming to an end."

Jim grinned as he replied, "Yeah, it's kinda' nice to finish up--if we can just get the plowing done."

"Oh, I think we'll get it done, and if we don't, it won't be that serious," John continued. "Say, I think I'll pull the plug if you want to stay here and finish up."

"Sure, I'll wind it up, John. You go ahead," the young man replied cheerfully.

John Schneidermann left the control building, walked to the truck cab, and opened the door. The big, black and silver shepherd looked out. "Come on, Fritz. Time to go." The dog bounced down the steps of the truck cab and followed behind his master. John Schneidermann walked over to where a dark blue pickup truck was parked. He brushed off the accumulated snow, climbed into the cab, and started the engine. The snow was still coming down as he pulled out of the elevator site and onto the highway. After about five miles, he turned off the highway and onto a gravel road. In three more miles, he turned in at a farmstead.

John Schneidermann pulled into a garage stall after raising the door with a remote opener. "Come on, Fritz, we'll call it a day."

The dog leaped out of the pickup. The farmer walked the short distance to the large, square, two-story farmhouse and opened the back door. In the spacious entryway, he removed his wet sweatshirt, gloves, cap, and boots.

"Is that you, John?" A female voice came from the kitchen. "How did it go today?"

"Oh, the snow made us quit, but we're on the last field," John responded.

"There is some supper on the table," the woman announced.

"That sounds great. I'll be right there," John answered as he turned into a small bathroom just off the entryway. The farmer washed his hands, looked into the mirror, and lightly combed his thinning hair. Across from the bathroom was an office, and beyond was the door to the kitchen. In the kitchen, the farmwife had set the table with white china and stainless-steel utensils. She placed some fried potatoes, ham, a salad, and cooked corn on the table in serving dishes.

John Schneidermann sat down to the table and leaned back. "I am a little tired tonight. It feels good to relax."

He began filling his plate from the china serving dishes in the middle of the chrome and Formica kitchen table.

The woman was tall and slim with blue eyes and slightly graying hair. She spoke with a pleasant voice, "We received a letter from Dan today."

"Is that so."

She continued, "Yes, you can read it after supper. He says he is coming home for the holidays."

"That sounds good," John spoke between bites.

The trim farm lady spoke again in a steady voice, "He said he has changed his thinking about farming."

"Really." John Schneidermann looked up in mild surprise. The mother continued, "He said he would like to discuss the farming situation with you."

"That sounds interesting," John Schneidermann remarked as he looked up at his wife. "Is there any other mail?" he asked.

"I put it on the desk."

John Schneidermann finished his supper and got up from the table. He walked across the kitchen floor toward the office. As he went by the farmwife, he gave her an affectionate slap. "Good supper, dear."

The office was comfortable with its knotty pine paneling, cork tile flooring, and spacious windows with a view of the yard and grove. On one side was a blonde oak desk with a matching chair. On the wall above the desk was a large, framed picture of a smiling young man in a tan uniform and the polished brown cavalry boots of a Texas A&M cadet. Another wall held a framed piece of green felt. Several badges and emblems lay on the cloth under the glass: gold bars, U.S. crossed rifles, the black and red patch of the 7th Infantry Division, a blue regimental shield with red and white markings, a silver and blue combat infantry badge, two rows of ribbons. In a lower desk drawer, in a walnut case, was a .45 automatic pistol. The finish of the weapon showed several scratches and some worn spots from being carried in a holster.

# Teamwork

The pickup truck kicked up a trail of dust as it rolled down the gravel road. John Schneidermann was making a hurried trip to where one of his tractors was plowing under the remains of corn stalks after the combines had gone through. The weather had been cold and wet, but it had changed and was in the process of drying out. Up ahead and to the right, in a field of broken corn stalks was a stationary tractor and plow. The pickup pulled up beside the massive machine. The tractor was a huge four-wheel drive unit. With eight tires, each over six feet high, and a 300-horsepower engine, it was an impressive machine. The ten-bottom plow trailed behind for some twenty feet. The operator stood beside the plow and the idling tractor engine. The frost from the previous night covered the ground and the broken stubs of stalk.

"What's the problem, Jim?" the farmer asked.

"It's that stabilizer bar on the plow. It broke off right next to the threads," Jim quickly answered.

"Could be worse," John commented. "I brought along some cable and some clips. I think we will just take off the rod and replace it with the cable."

"That sounds good to me, John," the young operator replied as he started taking off the long, heavy, steel rod. Both men fished out the repair material from the pickup and began stringing it in place.

"Jim, tighten the clips, and I'll get out the torch," John directed.

John Schneidermann uncoiled a length of the dual green-and-red hose from the two gas cylinders mounted in the pickup box. Steadily and smoothly, he struck a spark igniting the acetylene side of the torch. The other side of the system poured a stream of oxygen, creating a clean, blue flame.

"I'll cut the cable, and we'll be in business," the older man announced. John Schneidermann, in a practiced motion, played the torch on the cable. As the cable turned red, he turned on an extra blast of oxygen. Amid a shower of sparks, the cable fell in two.

"Looks good, John. That should do it," Jim stated pragmatically. As the two men made a final check of their repair, the radios in the tractor and the pickup came to life.

"Unit 6. This is base. Come in.".

John Schneidermann reached through the open window of the pickup, picked up the handset, and pressed the talk button. "This is Unit 6. Go ahead."

The base announced, "I got a call from Johnson. Their combine just got stuck. Can we give them a pull?"

"Where are they at?"

"Over on their north place."

"I know where it is. It's only about three miles from us. Call them back and tell them we will be over with one of the four-wheel drives. I'll bring the big cable." John Schneidermann walked over to the tractor operator. "We better give them a pull. Let's unhook. You take the pickup over to the shop and get the big cable, and I'll meet you at Johnson's with the tractor."

The two men quickly pulled the several hydraulic hoses apart. The "quick disconnects" popped as they released. John slowly climbed into the cab of the giant tractor. As he gently edged the big machine back, Jim pulled the large draw pin that connected the tractor with the plow. The huge diesel roared to full RPMs as it started across the corn stalks toward the road. On the road the farmer shifted up and headed off at top speed, 18 MPH. The mud chunks from the tires flew into the air like a series of irregular missiles.

It was a beautiful time of the year. The air was clear and cool. The leaves were varied shades of red, tan, and yellow. The frost gave the trees, fences, and standing corn a lacy trim. Ahead of the tractor, a ring-necked pheasant walked majestically across the gravel road. The male bird's colorful plumage added a splash of brilliance to the scene.

John got out of the tractor cab and walked over to the men. "This doesn't look too bad, Myron," John remarked.

"Yeah, I guess it could be worse. These damn potholes! If a man would just have enough sense to stay out of them in the first place," the combine owner answered with a note of disgust.

"Jim will be here with the big cable in a few minutes. How do you want to handle this?" John queried.

"If you could get behind the machine, we'll hook onto the front axle, give it an easy pull, and I think that will do it," Johnson, the rangy farmer, directed.

"Sounds like a winner," John Schneidermann replied.

The combine was one of the largest made. Its partial load of shelled corn dramatically increased the overall weight of the machine. The pickup came into view as it topped a rise in the landscape. It turned off the road and bounced across the cornfield to where the combine and tractor were standing. As the pickup came to a halt, two of the men reached into the box and began unwinding the heavy wire rope with several feet of massive chain on each end. The men stretched out the cable, taking one end under the body of the combine. The end was carefully attached to the big box axle of the combine. John Schneidermann walked to the idling tractor and climbed the ladder to the cab. He then drove the massive eight-wheeled machine to a position directly behind and seventy feet back of the mired harvester. The other end of the cable was looped around the drawbar of the big tractor. The farmer, Johnson, walked to the tractor.

John Schneidermann opened the door of the tractor cab and called out, "I'll tighten the cable and then pull in my low gear and at an idle. That should do it."

Johnson replied, shouting above the sounds of the idling engines, "I'll get in the combine and help as much as possible. I'll flash my lights if I want you to stop." John Schneidermann replied with a nod, yet knowing that pulling a combine can be a risky operation. Serious damage can result--even cases of combines being pulled apart in an attempt to retrieve them from a soft spot.

The big tractor, with all eight tires in contact with firm ground, moved slowly ahead. The great cable, like a living being, snapped into a taut position. The men on the ground stepped back to a safer place as the huge tractor crept ahead. As if lifted by a giant hand, the great green combine lurched upward and backward out of its trapped condition. The tractor stopped, the cable slackened, and the combine moved back under its own power. Both machines stopped, and the men on the ground quickly unhooked the heavy cable and dragged it over to the pickup. The combine owner, Johnson, walked over to the tractor as John Schneidermann was climbing down from the cab.

"Thanks, John. I really appreciate it. Our nearest rig was twenty-five miles away," he stated, relieved and relaxed.

"No problem. I'm glad we could do it," John replied. As Jim came walking up, John gave a casual order, "Take the tractor back and see how our fix works."

John Schneidermann opened the door of the dark-blue pickup truck and climbed in. "Well, Fritz, that went pretty smooth," the farmer said as he reached over and scratched the big, black and silver shepherd behind the ears.

The four-wheel drive pickup, a heavy-duty half-ton, was equipped with a two-way radio, a toolbox that sat across the box just behind the cab, and a set of gas welding tanks. He picked up the radio handset pressing the "talk" button. "I'll give you a hand hooking up, Jim."

"OK, John," Jim's voice came through the receiver.

John Schneidermann engaged the starter of the pickup and started across the cornfield toward the gravel road. The pickup came to the road and turned in the direction of the departing tractor. In a few minutes, the form of the giant tractor could be seen ahead as it was turning into the field. The four-wheel drive tractor made its way across the field of broken stalks toward the standing plow. Jim swung the machine into position directly ahead of the plow. The pickup followed the massive machine and parked beside the plow. John Schneidermann opened the door, got out, and walked to the rear of the tractor.

As he lifted the heavy tongue of the plow, Jim carefully maneuvered the drawbar to allow the insertion of the hardened steel hitch pin. Jim briskly climbed down the ladder of the tractor and jogged to the rear of the machine. Both men worked silently together connecting the hydraulic hoses. In a few minutes the job was done, and Jim trotted to the left side of the tractor and scrambled up the ladder.

"We'll give her a try, John," Jim announced with a smile. The engine roared from an idle to full RPMs, and a plume of black smoke poured from the stacks. Slowly the unit started forward and then increased to full forward speed.

With deliberation, John Schneidermann walked back to the pickup, opened the door, and slid in behind the wheel, silently watching the plowing rig, with the power of 300 horses, make its pass down the field. The rich, black soil rolled from the steel moldboards creating a pattern of shining ribbons.

Jim's voice came again, crackling over the radio speaker, "I think our fix is going to work, John. I'll keep rolling and try to finish up this field."

John Schneidermann answered in radio parlance, "10-4."

The big machine kept up a steady movement back and forth, making turns on the ends of the field. As the plow approached the headland, the forward half with five bottoms would suddenly lift out of the earth, followed by the rear half. The ponderous machine turned with surprising agility and started on the next pass.

John William Schneidermann, son of the Northern Plains, gazed across the cornfield and beyond to the horizon. A distant row of towering cottonwood trees marked the location of a drainage ditch. Overhead a hawk circled, majestically riding on a current of air. Off to the right, a pair of white-tailed deer stepped cautiously across the gravel road and headed toward the shelter of an abandoned grove.

# Epilogue

In a far corner of Asia, by the shore of the Chosin, the cold winds of winter still blow over the mountains. The road still winds and twists along the eastern shore of the reservoir. It is peaceful now. Black war birds no longer fly, and track-mounted guns are silent. People tilling small patches of level land live there. There are houses and gardens. Trees grow on the slopes of the hills. On occasion, when the soil is disturbed, a reminder of past events may appear: a rusted bayonet, a shell fragment, or a cartridge case.

Along the ridges on the high ground are the remains of entrenchments and depressions in the earth covered over with grass. And, scattered throughout the valleys and the slopes where the battle was fought, hidden by the advance of time and nature, are the shallow graves of the men who fell there.

CPSIA information can be obtained
at www.ICGtesting.com
Printed in the USA
BVHW021736020223
657745BV00013B/480